HAM JONES

———

Ham Jones, Ante-Bellum Southern Humorist

◆ AN ANTHOLOGY ◆

Edited with an Introduction by

WILLENE HENDRICK AND

GEORGE HENDRICK

ARCHON

1990

First published 1990 as an Archon Book,
an imprint of The Shoe String Press, Inc.,
Hamden, Connecticut 06514

The paper used in this publication meets the
minimum requirements of American National
Standard for Information Science—Permanence
of Paper for Printed Library Materials,
ANSI Z39.48-1984 ⊚

Printed in the United States of America

Library of Congress Cataloging-in-Publication Data

Jones, Hamilton Chamberlain, 1798–1868
Ham Jones, ante-bellum Southern humorist:
an anthology / edited with an introduction by
Willene Hendrick and George Hendrick.
p.   cm.
Includes bibliographical references.
1. Humorous stories, American—Southern States.
2. Southern States—Fiction.   3. Southern States—Humor.
I. Hendrick, Willene, 1928–   II. Hendrick, George.   III. Title.
PS2150.J78A6   1990
813'.3—dc20   89–18535
ISBN 0-208-02272-4

◆ CONTENTS ◆

v

Contents

INTRODUCTION

"Scattered through the South and Southwest," Franklin J. Meine wrote in his pioneering study *Tall Tales of the Southwest: An Anthology of Southern and Southwestern Humor 1830–1860*, "there sprang up a picturesque local-color group of humorists who flourished in barrooms, on law circuits, on steamboats and in the wide open spaces." One of the most engaging of these Southern humorists was Hamilton Chamberlain Jones (1798–1868), a well-educated, conservative attorney from the Piedmont area of North Carolina. He lived in a part of the state where there were a few families of wealth and position and thousands of ill-educated Tar Heels, many of whom were in need of his legal services. Beginning in 1831, Jones published a series of humorous stories drawn from characters and incidents he encountered in his varied legal and professional activities. These stories were to bring him local fame, though his identity was not known to the general American public. After his first story, entitled "Cousin Sally Dilliard," appeared, his later sketches were signed "By the author of 'Cousin Sally Dilliard,' " without identifying Jones by name.

As Meine perceptively noted, the "early humor of the South . . . was distinctly and peculiarly Southern; and it was provincial, wholly local."[1] Ham Jones (as he was known to his friends) knew the classic authors of Greece and Rome and England; as his obituary, probably written by a family member, noted: "With him literature was a passion. Possessed of a fine critical taste and a remarkably retentive memory he stored his mind with a rich fund of classical and literary knowledge.[2] The subject matter for his sketches, however, was local and based on careful observations of his North Carolina world. During his lifetime, his sketches were widely reprinted and copied and retold by storytellers anonymous and famous ("Cousin Sally Dilliard" is said to have been a favorite of Lincoln's),[3] but after his death his fame diminished, probably because his stories were scattered in newspapers and journals and therefore hard for readers to find or to identify as his.

Jones in many respects conforms to the biographical archetype of the Southern and Southwestern humorist as outlined by Kenneth S. Lynn in *Mark Twain and Southwestern Humor*: "A professional man— a lawyer or a newspaperman. . . . He was actively interested in politics, either as a party propagandist or as a candidate for office. He was well educated. . . . Above all, he was a conservative, identified either with the aristocratic faction in state politics, or with the banker-oriented Whig party in national politics, or with both."[4] Jones certainly fits all the outer shapes of that mold, but conservative though he was he had doubts about the nullification movement, about the institution of slavery, and about the necessity of going to war in 1861. Member of a prominent social and political family, he admired the richly inventive language of Tar Heels and generally presented, without authorial disapproval, the disruptive and antisocial behavior of the poor whites in his state. His sketches are subversive, holding up to ridicule the very institutions he and his class consciously upheld.

Jones began to publish and became well known as "The Author of 'Cousin Sally Dilliard' " at the same time that the Down East Humorists—Seba Smith, creator of Jack Downing; Thomas Chandler Haliburton, author of the Sam Slick stories; James Russell Lowell, author of *The Biglow Papers*, which brought him to prominence; Frances M. Whitcher, creator of the garrulous Widow Bedott; and Benjamin Shillaber, author of the sketches about Mrs. Partington—were coming to prominence. Ham Jones published his own newspaper for many years and would have known of the work of some of these Down East Humorists through the "exchanges" he picked up from other papers and reprinted in his own newspaper.

Jones is more allied, however, with the Southern and Southwestern humorists—August Baldwin Longstreet, author of *Georgia Scenes* (1835); Johnson J. Hooper, author of *Adventures of Simon Suggs* (1845); William T. Thompson, creator of *Major Jones's Courtship* (1843) and other volumes about the Major—many of whom had stories appearing in *The Spirit of the Times*, where Jones was often published. These humorists were pioneers in American literary realism in their use of colloquial language; in their characterizations (for instance Yellow Blossom in Longstreet's "The Horse Swap," Simon Suggs in such stories as "The Captain Attends a Camp-Meeting"); in their presentation of religious, social, and political hypocrisy; and in their subversive presentation of people and events. Though Jones was influenced by the humorists of his time, he drew his material from the Tar Heel world he saw as an attorney in the antebellum South.

BIOGRAPHICAL SKETCH

Hamilton C. Jones was born in Greenville County, Virginia, on August 23, 1798, and brought to Stokes County, North Carolina, when he was an infant. The new home of the Jones family was just south of the Virginia border in what was then thought of as the western part of the state. Jones's father died not long after the move to the Old North State, and Mrs. Martha Loftin Jones then married Colonel James Martin (1742–1834), a member of a prominent family. He had seen active service during the Revolution and from all accounts was an intensely patriotic man who was active in local and state affairs. Upon the death of his first wife, he married the recently widowed Mrs. Jones, who had only one child, Hamilton. Col. Martin had ten children from his first marriage, and he and his second wife, Martha, had five children.

Col. Martin was a large landowner; his plantation on Snow Creek, where Hamilton C. Jones spent his childhood, contained 640 acres, and he held additional land in other parts of the state and in Tennessee. His brother, Alexander (1740–1807), was a member of the state delegation to the federal Constitutional Convention but departed before the Constitution was framed and did not sign it. Alexander had been governor of the state from 1781 to 1784 and again for three additional terms beginning in 1789. In 1792 he was elected to the U.S. Senate, but when he was not reelected six years later, he retired to his plantation in Rockingham County. Jones therefore had important political connections through the Martin family; he also fell in love with and married Col. Martin's granddaughter, Eliza, the child of Sarah Martin (the oldest child from the colonel's first marriage) and Major Pleasant Henderson. Through his marriage Jones became allied with the prominent Henderson family, with its many lawyers, doctors, and wealthy landowners.[5]

The Martin family was conservative politically, and Jones was to follow in that tradition. In a state that developed strong Republican sympathies, the Martins generally supported landed and monied interests. When Jones was a university student he supported the Federalists, and after the demise of that party, he was passionately committed to Whig principles.

In the Martin family there was a strong tradition for education not often present in other Southern families at that time. Both of Col. Martin's brothers had graduated from the College of New Jersey (now Princeton), and although he himself seems not to have attended college, he sent young Hamilton Jones to the Academy for boys at Chapel Hill to be prepared for entering the University of North Carolina. According to the *Raleigh Register* of 1812, there were four classes in the Academy:

> Every possible attention is paid to improvement in reading, writing, spelling and the English Grammar. Wm. Mimerall is now a resident of Chapel Hill for the purpose of teaching the French language, and is well qualified. The sessions run as follows: The first from 1st of January to 24th of May. The second from the 20th June to the 15th of November. The expenses are for the first session in the dining-room and College, Diet, $30; Tuition, $10; Room-rent, $1; Servant hire, $1.50; Library, 50 cents; Washing, $8; candles and wood, $4; Bed, $3.50; Total, $58.50. For the second session, the same. Plainness of dress and manners will be the rule.

Although the *Register* did not emphasize this aspect of the curriculum, the course of study was also heavily classical: the students preparing to enter the university were charged to know Latin and Greek grammar and to have mastered such texts as *Aesop's Fables, Caesar's Commentaries,* six books of the *Aeneid,* and St. John's Gospel and the Acts of the Apostles in Greek.[6] Jones entered the university in 1814, and given the requirements for college admission he must have spent several terms at the preparatory school in Chapel Hill. In the university, he continued to pay the same fees as when he had been enrolled in the academy—$117 for two terms.[7]

Most American colleges at the end of the eighteenth century were sectarian, and the concept of state universities was a new one. The University of Georgia was the first state university to gain a charter (January 27, 1785), but the University of North Carolina was the first to open its doors—on January 15, 1795. The trustees held their first regular meeting in November of 1790, and Alexander Martin, who was then governor of the state, became the president of the board. Chapel Hill was chosen as the site for the new university. The contract for the first structure on campus—East Building, containing classrooms and living quarters for the students—was signed in 1793. The building for the preparatory school was completed in 1802. A few other buildings were soon built and in 1812 the *Raleigh Register* reported that

> In six months the Principal (South) Building [known as Main Building] will be ready for the reception of inhabitants. [Completion was actually delayed until 1814.] There will then be accommodations for eighty students. There will be separate halls for the Dialectic and Philanthropic Societies, one for the Library, and a Public Hall for Prayers. Each of the Society libraries contains 800 to 1,000 volumes, that of the University 1,500, a total of 3,100 to 3,500 volumes. . . . The Faculty consists of a President, three Professors and one Tutor.[8]

Much of Jones's intellectual and social life, and that of his fellow students, revolved around the societies; he belonged to the Dialectic Society, and its library, its debates, its meetings were important to this conservative, well-connected young man. It was undoubtedly fortunate that the societies were flourishing, for by 1817, Jones's junior year, the university had a remarkably small teaching staff.

During the fall term, President Caldwell and one principal tutor, assisted by other lesser tutors, made up the entire faculty of the college. The student body during these years was small also, generally about one hundred.

Campus problems had been developing for a number of years. The respected president of the institution, Dr. Joseph Caldwell, in 1812 requested to be allowed to step down as chief administrator in order to return to teaching and to resume research, and he was replaced by Dr. Robert H. Chapman, a Presbyterian minister. Dr. Chapman assumed his new duties in 1813, during the War of 1812, but he was an ardent Peace Federalist and did not support the war, as most of the students did. He made no attempt to hide his beliefs, and feelings ran high on the campus. Those ill feelings remained after the war was over, and some "outrages" were "perpetrated on his property": cutting the hair off the tail of his horse, hiding his cart, turning over a house (probably a privy), and removing a gate from its hinges and carrying it away. The president was unwilling to ignore the pranks, and according to Kemp P. Battle,* who wrote the magisterial *History of the University of North Carolina,* Dr. Chapman "applied to a Justice of the Peace, Major Pleasant Henderson [later to be Jones's father-in-law], for a warrant against the unknown perpetrators, intending to call up all the students and examine them on oath." Major Henderson resisted, for he had found those general warrants to be unlawful, but, Dr. Battle's account continued, "the fiery doctor, who could be no more easily diverted from his purpose than a well-trained bloodhound from the track of a fleeing criminal, amended the precept by inserting the names of five students." The resulting trial was a travesty with unpleasant consequences for the five students whose names were entered in the warrant. A large number of students were called to testify. Some were vociferous in their statements that they knew nothing about the incident but others, as Battle notes, "gave the names of suspected persons, some of whom were undoubtedly not guilty. . . . The Justice's examination violated all the rules of evidence. Leading questions were asked, the witnesses were required to give their

*Proper names and words appearing in the glossary are identified by an asterisk the first time they appear in the text.

6

suspicions, and hearsay evidence was even admitted as to what suspicions were entertained by others, and as to what students knew of any of the perpetrators." Although the records were lost, Battle believed that all five students were dismissed from the university.[9] There is no record of Jones's reaction to these proceedings, but he must have been personally distressed, for as a Federalist he would have supported the president, but as an ardent believer in the Constitution he could hardly have supported the outrageous legal conduct of the president and the justice of the peace.

In another incident involving a conflict between Dr. Chapman and students at the university, Jones is known to have supported the president and the trustees in a political struggle. In September of 1816, Jones's junior year, William Biddle Shepard, a senior who came from a well-known New Bern family, submitted an oration to the president, as he was required to do, and Dr. Chapman, following a right granted to him by the trustees, deleted some favorable comments about the Republican party and instructed Shepard not to deliver those comments in his public speech. Shepard, however, ignored the order, and began to deliver his speech as he had written it. Dr. Chapman ordered him to desist, but Shepard continued, and many students called out "Go on! go on!" The next day, a large number of students met in the chapel and passed resolutions upholding Shepard's conduct and their own. The faculty of the university, however, strongly supported the president. Shepard and several students who were his staunch supporters were suspended, and all those students who had met in the chapel were forced to acknowledge "that those who applauded Shepard were guilty of gross disorder and disrespect of authority; . . . that on the next morning they transgressed their duty as students and as good members of society, by proceeding with tumultuous noise and riotous behavior to the Public Hall, and uniting in an unlawful and disorderly assembly for the purpose of opposing the Faculty and violating the laws; . . . that they hoped for forgiveness and solemnly promised faithfully to submit to the laws of the University and deport themselves as orderly members of society." Jones (and many other conservative, orderly students) signed the resolution. Battle seems to have had considerable sympathy for the students involved in the affair, but after reviewing all the evidence, he came to the conclusion that "the President is not censurable for enforcing a law of the Trustees forbidding political speeches."[10]

Jones the conservative could support the actions of the university president without hesitation, for the president had authority for his actions against a Republican student. In February of 1817, following the events of the previous September, Jones wrote in a letter, "Shepard and Dromgolle [one of Shepard's strongest supporters] are very much censured by all the sober part of the community. Shepard's speech has lost its popularity, and notwithstanding the great puffing of the New Bern editor has been stigmatized by every judge of literary merit as a flowery piece of nonsense." He went on to report that the Dialectic Society, to which he belonged, "is still in a very flourishing condition." He noted that the other society on campus, the Philanthropic, to which Shepard belonged, "though increasing in numbers, degenerates in point of talent." Kemp Battle understood the political implications of Jones's letter and bluntly noted: "The writer . . . though the Federalist party was practically extinct, sympathized with its principles, and afterwards followed Clay into the wigwam of the Whigs, while Shepard continued to be a warm Republican and became Democratic leader."[11]

Thoroughly unpopular on campus, President Chapman resigned, and Dr. Caldwell again resumed that office. Course offerings must have been severely limited in 1817; because of the turmoil the entire staff of the university was reduced to the president and one principal tutor, William Hooper, assisted by two other tutors. Hooper, who had become tutor in 1812, was called to the chair of ancient languages in 1818, and Elisha Mitchell arrived in Chapel Hill early that year to fill the chair vacated by Dr. Caldwell. The following year Dr. Shepard Kollock was called to the chair of rhetoric. Jones would undoubtedly have studied Greek and Latin with Hooper, and mathematics with Dr. Caldwell and perhaps also with Elisha Mitchell. Dr. Mitchell, a descendant of John Eliot, the Apostle to the Indians, had been a classmate of A. B. Longstreet (author of *Georgia Scenes*) at Yale.[12] Jones probably also delved into moral philosophy with Dr. Caldwell. Though the curriculum was, by modern standards, restricted, the students were expected to augment their formal education through their literary societies.

Southern college students were generally rowdy, and Dr. Battle in his history of the university lists the offences charged to one student in 1818: "Torturing animals with spirits of turpentine," "lying," "slandering the Faculty," "threatening physical violence to a member of the Faculty," "writing scurrilous and abusive stuff on the Chapel walls about the same," and "drawing a dirk on a student."[13] Not surprisingly, there were consistent efforts to keep the young men occupied and out of mischief. Lectures took most of the morning and afternoons. After lectures were concluded, there was alloted time for recreation, but the students were to be in their rooms by eight in the winter and by nine during the summer. Public examinations were held at the end of each term.

In a letter of August 14, 1816, Jones wrote that the business of the Dialectic Society had been more orderly and regular "since the repeal of the law compelling members to attend public prayers under penalty of a fine." He went on to describe one debate topic before the society: "do we experience more pleasure from contemplating the works of nature or of art." He argued "that the greater pleasure arises from viewing the works of nature, because no painter nor sculpturer can produce in the mind of man that exquisite sensation which is produced in the mind of the lover from contemplating the fascinating charms of his dulcinea. I have many other arguments to advance in corroboration of my subject but that drawn from the beauties of a fair one preponderates with me, and I doubt not will weigh considerably with one whose heart has been perforated by the darts of Cupid." Jones won the question, and he was to win the hand of the "fair one," Eliza Henderson.[14]

The study of languages and the emphasis on debates and orations obviously were good training for Jones in his later career as a lawyer. He was also undoubtedly much influenced by Dr. Caldwell, one of the most impressive members of the faculty. Dr. Caldwell was in charge of the study of natural philosophy, roughly equivalent to natural sciences, and he emphasized the "order and harmony of creation." He had been a student of John Witherspoon at the College of New Jersey, and like his mentor, also a Presbyterian clergyman, he defended religious orthodoxy.[15] This Presbyterian orthodoxy may not have had strong appeal to Jones, who was an Episcopalian, as were the Martins. With the arrival of Elisha Mitchell from Yale, scientific studies were more in the modern tradition.

The graduating class of 1818 was a distinguished one. First in the class was James Polk, who was to become president of the United States. Second honors went to William Mercer Green, later bishop of Mississippi and chancellor of the University of the South. Third honors went to Robert Hall Morrison, later to be president of Davidson College. Fourth honors went to Hamilton C. Jones. The commencement ball was apparently a colorful one. Gen. Mallett recalled his dress, and we can assume Ham Jones was similarly attired:

> My coat was broadcloth, of sea-green color, high velvet collar to match, swallow-tail, pockets outside with lapels, and large silver-plated buttons; white satin damask vest, showing the edge of a blue under-vest; a wide opening for bosom ruffles, and no shirt collar. The neck was dressed with a layer of four or five three-cornered cravates, artistically laid and surmounted with a cambrick stock, pleated and buckled behind. My pantaloons were white canton crape, lined with pink muslin, and showed a peach-blossom tint. They were rather short in order to display flesh-colored silk stockings, and this exposure was increased by very low cut pumps with shiny buckles.[16]

The fourteen gentlemen who graduated that year were quite likely accompanied by belles also as suitably and elegantly attired. The graduating students at the University of North Carolina were clearly the sartorial and economic elite of the state.

Jones was apparently well thought of by Dr. Caldwell and the faculty, for he was asked to stay on as tutor during the 1818–1819 academic year. He held that position for only a year, and it may be that he found the disciplinary problems facing a tutor not entirely to his liking. Dr. Battle recounts this anecdote:

> At the time when Hamilton C. Jones . . . was a tutor in the University, disorder in the classes and disrespect to the members of the Faculty were fashionable, the result of treating students like

school-boys. Jones told his classes that he would treat them as
gentlemen, and expected corresponding behavior towards himself.
Pretty soon a student of stalwart muscle offered the teacher some
rudeness. Jones requested him to wait a moment after the close of
the exercises. He then proposed a walk into the forest, and on the
bully's refusal to apologize and promise amendment, gave him a fair
fight and a sound thrashing. He had no further trouble in the matter
of discipline. [17]

For whatever reason, Jones did not choose the academic life;
instead, he decided to study law in New Bern with William Gaston
(1778–1844), a staunch Federalist and the most distinguished
attorney in the state. Given Gaston's eminence, Jones chose the
right man with whom to associate himself, but the decision was not
without its dangers, for Gaston was a Catholic in a state strongly,
even rabidly, anti-Catholic. At that time, the state constitution
forbade anyone who denied "the Truth of the Protestant religion"
from holding civil office in the state. [18] Jones's career did not suffer,
however, from his close association with a Catholic, and his choice
of a law teacher shows him to be both independent and not always
conventional.

Jones wrote Professor Mitchell a long letter from New Bern soon
after he had taken up his new studies, and the tone would indicate
that Mitchell and Jones were friends: "Newbern, I suppose, is more
remarkable for talents than any part of North Carolina. Mr. Gaston,
accounted the greatest man in our State, I find one of the most mild
and unassuming gentlemen of my acquaintance." During his stay
in New Bern, Jones was acting as tutor to the two sons of Josiah
Howard, a wealthy planter: "I have lately returned from a visit to
Howard's country seat. He has a most extensive farm, and has it
managed more to my notion of the business than any one I ever
saw. He is indeed the most curious compound of good and bad
qualities that I ever knew—extremely kind to his friends, but most
bitter against his enemies. His wife is a good and even-tempered
woman. His boys, tho' I make them study closely, can never be
made scholars. They are quite easily managed and give me no
trouble except at their recitations twice in the day." Dr. Battle, in
his gloss on the letter, did not comment on the lack of scholarly

interest shown by the Howard boys but observed dryly that they became planters.

In the letter to Mitchell, Jones also mentioned another incident that remains somewhat obscure. He gave this description of his recent trip from Raleigh to New Bern:

> The road . . . leads through a country remarkable for little else than its dismal, inhospitable appearance. The growth consists chiefly in long-leaf pines which grow so closely together that I was reminded all the way along "of the shadow of the Valley of Death," and, when I had the misfortune to lose "my siller and gear," my imagination partook so much of horror that hung around me, until I wished for some friendly opiate to keep me insensible till I could get to Newbern. The sameness of this appalling scene was uninterrupted, except by a miserable lightwood-smoked hovel now and then, which only served to kindle the apprehension that I should have to lodge in one of the sort on the approaching night; and to my unutterable chagrin I was not disappointed.

What happened? How did he lose his silver and his gear? Was he set upon by robbers? Did he have an accident when he was fording a river? He gives no answer. He also did not describe his two nights in the hovels. It is indeed unfortunate that this patrician, well-educated gentleman did not record for us his early experiences among the unwashed.

One other paragraph of Jones's letter to Dr. Mitchell is of particular note because of its comments on politicians who dueled and because it is a forerunner of his interest in the predicaments of uneducated North Carolinians caught in the coils of the law. In the first part of the paragraph he wrote of John Stanly, Federalist member of Congress, who shot and killed Richard Spaight, former governor of the state. After that shooting Stanly was pardoned. Jones wrote,

> I believe that you have formed a correct opinion in regard to J. Stanly. He is no doubt a man of first abilities, and shows quite plainly that he knows it. He is quite a useful citizen, has the confidence of all Newbern in almost everything, for he seems well acquainted with all kinds of business. He is much of a courtier in his manners and, of course, is a favorite with all the ladies. Stanly cannot

be blamed much for killing Spaight, for every one says he did every thing in his power to avoid the duel. They both fought to please the people, a majority of whom, being Democrats, would have shouted for joy if Stanly could have been killed. I have several anecdotes to tell you of Stanly's sprightliness of thought. On one occasion in the court a fellow gave evidence so pointedly against him that he knew of no other way to invalidate it than by impeaching his [the witness's] respectability. He accordingly told the court that the man had been guilty of stealing pork. This the witness took in dudgeon, and as Stanly came down the steps of the court-house the fellow met him with his fist clinched. "Stanly," says he, "how came you to say I stole pork?" "I said you stole pork?" "Yes, sir, you did," says the fellow. "You must be mistaken, sir." "You did, sir, and I can prove it by everybody in court." "Well, if I did, sir, I ask your pardon for the mistake, for I meant—bacon." This confounded the fellow so that Stanly had time to make his escape without molestation. It appears that his charge was true, for the fellow had actually stolen bacon.[19]

In this, and in later stories such as "Cousin Sally Dilliard," the legal world is presented ambiguously: it appears that the witness may well have been telling the truth but is vulnerable because of his past conduct. In the anecdote Stanly makes a shrewd guess and impeaches the credibility of the witness. The attorney is a gentleman, though somewhat soiled; the witness is unwashed and a thief. But is justice served? Jones presents the world as it is and does not moralize, and in doing so he subverts the established order. Even before he became a licensed attorney, Jones liked the storytelling world of country lawyers, and while the stories were entertaining and comic they almost always dealt with moral ambiguities.

In his letter to Professor Mitchell, Jones made a passing reference to the young lady with whom he was in love, noting "it is not good for man to be alone." Soon after he obtained his license to practice law in 1820, he married Eliza Henderson, the only daughter of Major Pleasant Henderson, and the young couple moved to Salisbury, where Jones began his law practice. The Martins had connections in Salisbury; Alexander Martin had settled there when he first moved to North Carolina from Virginia, and there were many Henderson relatives in the village and in the county.

Rowan County had a diverse population. There was a large enclave of German farmers of the Lutheran faith. They were descendants of Hessians, who had come from Pennsylvania, and they were living in the eastern section of the county. The Scotch-Irish, who were generally Presbyterian, settled the western part of the county. Dr. Mitchell's granddaughter, Hope Summerell Chamberlain, who grew up in the village, noted in her perceptive book, *This Was Home*, that there were several well-defined approaches to life in the community: "the English fashion, which was like the Virginia ideal—easy, assured, self-sufficient, traditional—was inherited by some who thought this the only sensible way—a way very definite for all its apparent freedom." A few families lived this way, including the Martins and the Joneses. They were landed people; they enjoyed the comforts of life and sporting events such as horse racing. They sent their sons to the University of North Carolina. The Hessian descendants were generally clannish, thrifty, and little concerned about formal education. The Scotch-Irish groups were puritanical; they believed in plain living and strong principles. The prosperous ones generally sent their sons to Davidson College.[20]

Rowan County had been prosperous immediately after the War of 1812, but the Panic of 1819 had wiped out much of that prosperity. Salisbury was still a village when the Joneses first settled there, and they found that they had come to an area already beginning to lose population and to show signs of stagnating, largely because of the high cost of transportation to this "Western" county. Still, during his first years in Salisbury Jones was able to establish a successful law practice, preside over a growing family—ten children (six of whom survived infancy) were born to the Joneses—and to build up a plantation, which he called "Como."

Ham Jones's early years in Salisbury were not, however, without their conflicts. He was a great admirer of his former law tutor William Gaston, a man of high principles and unimpeachable integrity. Gaston regularly took aspiring students into his office; one of his letters of advice to a former student has survived, and it is safe to assume that he gave much the same advice to Jones: "The qualifications which combine to make the illustrious lawyer are principally four. 1st. An intimate and thorough acquaintance with legal science. 2d. A facility in expressing his thoughts clearly, correctly, agreeably—and in so arranging and combining them in argument as to illustrate, convince, persuade. 3d. Unremitting attention to the interests of his clients. 4th. Incorruptible Integrity."[21] Gaston's advice on legal conduct and ethics was set forth in great detail, for he was aware that much law practice was conducted in county courts, where the suits were of a minor nature, and where it was difficult to keep from contracting bad habits. Judge Gaston was referring to that favorite pasttime of circuit-riding attorneys: retiring to the tavern for a convivial session of storytelling. It was in these sessions that Jones heard many of the stories he later wrote down and retold, but it was also this masculine, hard-drinking world about which Jones's mentor had grave doubts.

This conflict was not one Jones could easily resolve, and he talks passionately of it in a letter to Judge Gaston on July 2, 1829:

> The kindness of your letter to me of 29th of May affected me very deeply. I have wept with the bitterness of grief and shame at the retrospect which it held up to me. Alas Sir I tremble when I look back on my unprofitable life—and I tremble when I look forward lest I should not be able to resist the force of a dreadful and ruinous habit. *But I will make the effort* and I solemnly and deliberately make the promise to you to that effect. Since receiving yours I have been almost nauseated at the sight of spirits and feel stronger in the resolution I have made to renounce the use of the *ruinous* potion than I ever did before. The appeal which your letter made to my pride was and I hope will continue to give an energy to conduct which I have long been without. I will be candid with you even at the risk [of] incurring your contempt. When I first grew up I believed myself endowed with ability beyond most of my contemporaries. My success in life has been so little correspondent with these high wrought notions that I for a long time regarded them as the whisperings of vanity. It is this disappointment—this canker-worm in my hopes— that has brought me to what I was.

Jones went on to thank Judge Gaston for his interest, which he insisted would greatly influence his future life. While he undoubtedly did not remain a teetotaler the rest of his life, he did manage to gather his forces and become a well-known and respected attorney. In this letter we see him suffering self-doubts not usually associated with the early Southern humorists.

Jones also informed his mentor that his financial condition was almost desperate, for he had been surety for several of his friends who had experienced financial failures: "I shall have at the age of thirty one to begin the world anew with a considerable family." He had a plan, though, for recovering his fortunes. He was writing Judge Gaston from Callahan Mountain: "I have engaged pretty thoroughly in the Gold mining business and have succeeded so far as to strike a mine in two places of uncommon promise—no discovery had ever been made in this section of country before now in thirty miles of this place. Since however I have begun mines have been found in several places in the neighbourhood and there is abundant sign of this (the forks of the Yadkin) being the finest gold country in North Carolina." Jones, in the tradition of prospectors, was filled with hope: "I flatter myself that I have opened a vast resource and have certainly contributed to awaken a Spirit of enterprise and rescue the hopes of a community that with every advantage of soil &c had suffered & still is suffering by the change of times. God grant that my poor efforts may result in good to my fellow creatures—but it is still a hazzard and one on which I have much depending. My friend and relation Judge Martin has joined me & seems confident of success."[22] This claim was north of Salisbury and no appreciable amounts of gold were ever found at Callahan Mountain; the large strikes were at Gold Hill, south of the village.[23]

Though Jones was not to make his fortune at Callahan Mountain, the presence of the mining camp at Gold Hill, with all of the new wealth, the novelty of the operations, and the raw life of the white miners (slaves were also used at Gold Hill but their lives were more circumscribed), provided a boomtown atmosphere in a community near enough to Salisbury for him to observe it. A miner manqué himself, he missed his chance to deal with the rich subject that brought Mark Twain to national prominence.

Federalism was strongly entrenched in Salisbury, no doubt because it was the commercial and banking center for the area. The only newspaper in the village, the *Western Carolinian*, was firmly anti-Federalist and later anti-Whig. It was to become a powerful force for John C. Calhoun, following him into the nullification camp. Ham Jones was himself becoming interested in political journalism and was much opposed to the separatist movement. With the help of his stepbrother, Judge James Martin, and David F. Caldwell, the prominent political leader, Jones founded his own newspaper, *The Carolina Watchman*, to counter the political bent of the *Western Carolinian*. The first issue of Jones's paper appeared on July 28, 1832, and it was the aim of the editor, according to the "Prospectus" published in all the early issues, "to *instruct* and to *please*." He promised criticism and wit, and vowed to oppose the nullifiers. During the years he edited the newspaper, it was published in four pages. The first page contained the terms of subscription and advertising as well as political news—articles and speeches by leading politicians, generally—and a sprinkling of humorous stories. The second page was invariably given over to articles from the English and American exchanges, and, at times, letters from readers, often signed with fanciful noms de plume. The third page was devoted to local matters—leaders by the editor were generally on political matters, local, state, and national, and reflected Jones's strong Whig bias. During the nullification crisis, however, Jones was forced into support of Jackson because of the president's strong stand against the nullifiers. In the later years of his editorship he added local observations under the heading "Omnibus." Many of these humorous notes are similar to those regularly published in "The Talk of the Town" section in *The New Yorker*. The fourth page included at least one poem (Byron was a favorite, but popular New England poets were also included, as were Southern amateurs) and advertising (for bookstores, hotels, local academies, grocery and drygoods stores, estate sales, the return of runaway slaves). The paper was similar to most of the weeklies of the region but had many virtues not found in other country newspapers at that time: Jones's classical education and legal training contributed to the sharpness and literacy of his leaders, he had good taste in the exchange material he chose to include, and his comic sense was often evident in his pages. Jones was strong minded in political matters, and his opinions were ably argued and effective, but the inclusion of his humorous sketches—and those comic pieces picked up from the exchanges—lightened the tone of the paper.

Ham Jones's mentor, Judge Gaston, was philosophically opposed to slavery, and in an address in 1832 at the University of North Carolina, just one year after the Nat Turner insurrection, he called for "the ultimate extirpation of the worst evil that afflicts the Southern part of our Confederacy." He went on to assert "Disguise the truth as we may and throw the blame where we will, it is slavery which, more than any other cause, keeps us back in the career of improvement. It stifles industry and suppresses enterprise; it is fatal to economy and prudence; it discourages skill, impairs our strength as a community, and poisons morals at the fountain head."[24] From his long association with Judge Gaston, Jones would have known these views and he obviously shared them. In an editorial in the *Watchman* on January 19, 1833, Jones traced the origin of nullification to slavery, saying that having "absolute authority over a large number of our fellow beings is sure to beget a thirst of power and intolerance of civil rule." He went on to say that where only a few slaves were held, they were treated more humanely, and he asserted that the aristocracy and slavery were behind the movement for nullification.

Jones had more qualms about slavery than most of the Southern humorists, but as the abolitionist movement gained strength, his attitude shifted somewhat. To complicate his position he was himself a slave owner. In 1840 he had eleven slaves, six of whom were employed in agriculture; in 1850 he had eight slaves; in 1860 he was listed as having $4,600 in real estate and $14,863 in personal property. The latter figure may indicate that he still owned slaves, but through a mistake on the part of the census taker they may not have been listed in the slave schedule for 1860.[25] The evidence is not clear, and it is possible that he no longer had slaves by that date. By 1850 he was apparently unable to resist the fear of abolitionism that swept the South, even though he had once agreed with Judge Gaston's views. He may not have written the following article published in the *Carolina Watchman* on June 7, 1850, but it does seem to reflect his views in the decade before the Civil War:

> *Treatment of Slaves.*—Last Sabbath presented a scene, which, could Northern abolitionists have been here to witness it, must have

staggered their faith on the subject of the *horrors of slavery!*—Some weeks ago, a negro woman, the property of H. C. Jones, Esq., while engaged in cleaning up a piece of new ground, and burning the trash preparatory for the crop, her clothes taking fire, was so badly burned that her recovery, from the first, was despaired of. She however, lingered some two weeks and died. The Rev. Mr. Ricaud was invited to preach a funeral discourse at the plantation on Sabbath afternoon last, and notice to that effect was given out. At the appointed hour the slaves of this Town were seen moving out—not on *foot*, like beasts of burden, or like friendless, unrespected human wretches; but like genteel and able folk, in carriages, barouches, buggies, carryalls, on horse back, &c. It is estimated that there were some five hundred in attendance at the funeral. The masters and mistresses of these slaves had loan[ed] their horses and vehicles for the occasion. This is only one instance out of many going to show the kindness and humanity with which this population is treated in our midst. And if it were not for the excitement which Northern men manage to keep up on the subject of abolition, the man, in our midst, who should prove neglectful of the happiness of his slave, would very soon be made to feel the scorn of his better neighbors.

The abolitionists would not, of course, have ignored the circumstances of the woman's injury and death.

While Jones's views on the evils of slavery changed over the years, his support of the Whig party did not. During the years that he edited the *Carolina Watchman,* he vigorously argued against nullification. He quarreled mightily with the editor of the *Western Carolinian* and with other Democratic editors. In his farewell statement to his readers on August 2, 1839, when he announced that he had disposed of the paper, he wrote, "Seven long years have I battled for sound Whig principles: sometimes under the most unfavorable circumstances, and more than once when my list [of subscribers] was so small as not to justify the expense." Still, the paper must be counted a success because of the high quality of Jones's leaders and the exchange articles he chose to reprint, and, of course, because of the fine humorous pieces he published.

Jones's publishing activities were carried out in addition to his law practice and his political career. The "Western" counties of North Carolina (Salisbury was then considered to be in the West) were underrepresented in the legislature when Jones went there to live, and after establishing himself in law he ran for, and was elected to, the North Carolina House of Commons in 1827 and again in 1828. He was re-elected in 1838, while still editing his newspaper, and in 1840. His legislative work in Raleigh was apparently eminently satisfactory. John H. Wheeler noted,

> He was a faithful and active officer; and was considered a genial companion, full of wit. All his efforts in the legislature were enlightened by his exquisite genius and humor. His efforts in the Legislature in 1828 on the bill of Robert Potter to reduce the salary of judges, was considered as fatal to that agrarian project; his speech on the bill to prosecute the banks took a view of that question that excited the admiration of some of the ablest men in the house; and his speech on the bill to locate the Judges, was unanswerable in its argument, withering in its satire, and triumphant in its humor. [26]

In later years he held other important positions; he became solicitor for the sixth Judicial District in 1844, holding that position for eight years. He then became reporter for the North Carolina Supreme Court, holding that office until he resigned in 1864. In this latter position, he edited the reports of important cases for official publication. In 1854 he published *A Digest of Reported Cases Determined in the Supreme Court of North Carolina, from the Year 1845. . . to the Year 1853,* and from 1855 to 1863 he compiled *Reports of Cases in Equity Argued in the Supreme Court of North Carolina {1853–1863}.* He also published other legal reports during these years. Because of the demanding work at the state supreme court in Raleigh, he gave up his law practice in Salisbury.

Jones's humorous sketches must have been written in odd hours during his busy life as a lawyer, newspaper editor, legislator, plantation owner, and head of a household with six children. Amidst all this activity, he began to write and publish humorous pieces in the early 1830s. His first story, "Cousin Sally Dilliard," appeared in *Atkinson's Saturday Evening Post* in 1831. He was well known in Salisbury as an author published not only locally but also in the *Saturday Evening Post* and in the famous sporting magazine *The Spirit of the Times* and then reprinted by way of exchanges throughout the country. *The Spirit of the Times* reprinted "Cousin

Sally Dilliard" several times and also published other stories by Jones: "McAlpin's Trip to Charleston," "Going to Muster in North Carolina," "The Sandy Creek Literary Society," "The Round Robin," "The Frenchman and His Menagerie," and "Abel Hucks in a Tight Place."

It was not only his fame that made him a popular figure, however. Dr. Battle characterized Jones as "an excellent *raconteur.*" Dr. Battle's father, who graduated from the university in 1820 and knew Jones well, reported that "often at social gatherings in his younger days the dancing room would be deserted, while all the company would form a circle around Ham Jones, as he recited with inimitable humor 'Cousin Sally Dillard' and other stories."[27] Another account suggests that Jones's popularity outside of North Carolina was considerable. During a Northern visit, Jones stopped in Baltimore and went to the theatre. The memorialist wrote,

> The piece enacted was a deeply impressive tragedy, which left the audience in a sad and sorrowful mood. They sat in silence awaiting the preparations for the farce for which few had any relish and on which many were about to turn their backs—when a whisper passed around, "The author of 'Cousin Sally Dillard' is in the house." Those who had risen to leave the theatre returned to their seats; eyes brightened, and a call loud and commanding was heard from every quarter for "Cousin Sally Dillard." The author was hurried by his friends *nolens volens** before the curtain, and such a scene as followed is seldom witnessed on the boards of any theatre. He was in "story telling" mood, and just in the right mood to discourse of "Cousin Sally," and the way he did tell that simple, but celebrated story of his own making was a caution to all play going people. Suffice it to say they laughed, cried, roared, beat the benches, encored and finally broke up in a row. The farce being suspended by the story, was not called for, the deep laid affecting scenes of the tragedy was forgotten, but while memory lasts the looks, gestures and dry humor of "Ham Jones" in the simple recital of that very simple story will remain, fresh and green, in the minds of all who heard him."[28]

Ham Jones seems to have had the same remarkable storytelling abilities and stage presence that were to make Mark Twain famous a generation later, but Jones continued his law career rather than taking to the lecture circuit, as Mark Twain did. Perhaps the nation in the late 1840s and 1850s was not yet ready to support Southern and Southwestern humorists as public performers. Jones, then, must be judged on the basis of his published stories, and we can agree with Franklin J. Meine in his assertion that " 'Cousin Sally Dilliard' takes its place along with Mark Twain's early masterpiece 'The Jumping Frog,' as one of the great American humorous stories."[29]

From those terrible years just before the war began, there is one pleasant and even restful episode to report in the life of Ham Jones. In the spring of 1856 David Hunter Strother, who wrote under the name of "Porte Crayon," came to Rowan County while he was doing an article on North Carolina for *Harper's*. He went to Gold Hill where he observed the mining operations and made various sketches to illustrate his article. He attended a May Day picnic near Salisbury, a celebration at which Jones was also present. Jones and Strother formed a mutual admiration society and exchanged anecdotes. On the third of May the celebrants took the train to Holtsburg, but instead of dancing on the green, they turned the train station into a festive hall. Bales of hay were moved into the building to serve as tables and seats. Picnic food was devoured. Corks from champagne "flew about like shot in a sharp skirmish." Though the two men had met only a few days earlier, they were completely comfortable with each other. Strother wrote in his notebook on April 28 that he had visited Jones and that he should include in his papers "the Debating Society story, the Kentucky Cobbler and wife, cock fights, the Red Negro." The notes for these stories are not in the Strother papers, and Jones's manuscripts can not be located. Strother's biographer does attribute part of a debating society story to Jones. That story is set in Tennessee, and it is not possible to determine how much of it should be ascribed to Jones, since all of Jones's known stories are set in North Carolina.[30]

The last years of Jones's busy and productive life must have been difficult ones indeed. When the war neared, his antinullification stand of almost thirty years previous must have haunted him. In fact, we know from an article entitled "Union Meeting" in the *Carolina Watchman* for January 1, 1861, that Jones felt there were constitutional avenues yet to be explored—that secession "was revolutionary and totally unsustained by the present state of facts." Reluctantly he decided that "after exhausting all efforts for a peaceable solution of the negro question, according to the forms of law within the Union, and there was no redress and guaranties obtained, he would then go with those who now advocated disunion, and would freely encounter all the horrors which by a forcible settlement seemed to him inevitable." His position was conservative and perfectly in harmony with his abhorrence of nullification, but the inevitable did happen. The *Carolina Watchman* reported on May 9, 1861, that Burton Craige, an ardent believer in secession, and H. C. Jones were nominated to represent Rowan County at the state convention being called to consider secession. The reasons behind the nominations were explained in the *Carolina Watchman* for July 22, 1861: the two political parties in the county agreed that each would be represented at the state convention because it would harmonize "the feelings of our people" and unite "them in the most vigorous efforts to promote the common cause of defence against the invaders of our soil." Whatever discomforts Ham Jones may have felt, he signed the Ordinance of Secession. Jones's obituary in the *Watchman & Old North State* for September 17, 1868, declared that "throughout the entire war [he] was earnest and zealous in its support." The statement is undoubtedly true.

He remained as reporter for the state supreme court through the early years of the war, resigning in 1864, but his wartime years must have been emotionally draining. He had two sons who served as officers in the Confederate Army; both survived, but Hamilton C. Jones, Jr., had many close calls. The *Watchman* on May 19, 1862, reported that Capt. H. C. Jones had been dangerously wounded, being shot through both thighs, at the battle of Williamsburg, and that Capt. Jones's father had him in his charge. Upon his recovery, he was promoted to the rank of colonel. At Rappahannock River on November 7, 1863, he was captured and imprisoned in the Old Capitol Prison and then on Johnson's Island in Lake Erie. He survived prison and was exchanged in February of 1865, immediately rejoined his regiment, and was again wounded in an attack on Fort Stedman.[31] The Joneses had all the anxieties of parents with sons at war, and in addition their own lives were unsettled. Jones had realized that the war would be horrible, and most of his fears came true. Goods and food became scare, inflation was rampant, the Confederate prison in Salisbury made the citizens fear for their safety, and in April of 1865, General George Stoneman and his Union forces occupied Salisbury. Seven thousand bales of cotton and much Confederate property were burned, but private homes were not destroyed. The war was over just as Salisbury was occupied.[32]

James S. Brawley in *The Rowan Story* characterized Salisbury spirit at the end of the war: "After years of sorrow, suffering and tension, emotion of any kind is soon exhausted. The feelings of the citizens of Rowan passed into numbness, and the people accepted the bare realism of defeat with stoic complacence. The courts continued to operate as they did in the half-century before; wills and transfers of land were probated."[33] There is no record that Hamilton C. Jones resumed his previous pursuits after the war was over; he published no stories, and we have no indication that he was active in a law practice, but his son Col. Jones opened a law office in Salisbury and perhaps the son solicited advice from his elderly father. On July 3, 1868, the *Watchman and Old North State* reported the death of Mrs. Jones, a consistent communicant of the Episcopal Church, and on September 17 of that year the paper carried the obituary of Hamilton Jones. He had died, the report stated, on September 10 at the home of his son-in-law, Dr. Samuel Tate, in Morganton, North Carolina. His obituary asserted that he left no enemies and that he was kind and considerate and charitable to the poor "both from impulse and from the teachings of that religion he professed and the comforts of which he enjoyed to the last years of his life." He had, in his early years in Salisbury, been on the Episcopal Church building committee and had been active in church affairs all during the time he lived there. Como passed out of the hands of the Jones family, and the house was destroyed in a fire in 1873.

Hamilton C. Jones's fame as a humorist has been almost forgotten in this century, though Mark Twain and other frontier humorists such as Augustus Baldwin Longstreet, Joseph G. Baldwin, George W. Harris, and others have continued to be popular. This book-length collection of Jones's humor will, we hope, introduce him to a new generation of readers and storytellers.

NOTES

1. Franklin J. Meine, ed., *Tall Tales of the Southwest: An Anthology of Southern and Southwestern Humor 1830–1860* (New York: Knopf, 1930), pp. xv–xvi. Meine's extensive collection of American humor is now in the Rare Book and Special Collections Library of the University of Illinois.
2. *Watchman & Old North State*, September 17, 1868, p. 2.
3. Van Wyck Brooks, *The Times of Melville and Whitman* (New York: Dutton, 1953), p. 234.
4. Kenneth S. Lynn, *Mark Twain and Southwestern Humor* (Westport, Conn.: Greenwood Press, 1975), p. 52.
5. For biographical information about the Martin family and Hamilton C. Jones, we have used *The Heritage of Stokes County, North Carolina* (Germanton, N.C.: Stokes County Historical Society, 1981), pp. 362–363; James McLachlan, *Princetonians 1748–1768* (Princeton, N.J.: Princeton University Press, 1976); the obituary of Hamilton C. Jones, *Watchman & Old North State*, September 17, 1868, p. 2; Richard Walser, "Ham Jones: Southern Folk Humorist," *Journal of American Folklore* 78 (October–December 1965); 295–316.
6. Kemp P. Battle, *History of the University of North Carolina, 1789–1868* (Raleigh, N.C.: Edwards and Broughton, 1907), I, 230. Information about studies preparatory to entering the University of North Carolina is drawn from the university catalog of 1819, reproduced in William S. Powell, *The First State University: A Pictorial History of the University of North Carolina* (Chapel Hill: University of North Carolina Press, 1972), p. 43.
7. Information supplied by Michael G. Martin, Jr., University of North Carolina archivist, in a letter dated February 21, 1984.
8. Battle I, 230; for general information about the University, Battle I, 1–283 and Powell, pp. 3–44.
9. Battle, I, 230–241.
10. Ibid.
11. Ibid., 239.
12. Ibid., 250–251.
13. Ibid., 262. Jones's half brother, Henry Martin, was a participant in a brutal fight in 1820; see Battle, I, 266–267.
14. Letter of H. C. Jones to Major Abraham Staples, August 14, 1816, Manuscripts Department, University of North Carolina at Chapel Hill Library; Charles Sellers, *James K. Polk: Jacksonian* (Princeton, N.J.: Princeton University Press, 1957), pp. 44–45.
15. Sellers, p. 46.

16. Battle, I, 258, 268–269.
17. "Letter of Hamilton C. Jones the Elder," edited by Kemp Battle, *North Carolina University Magazine* XXIII (April 1893): 216.
18. William Gaston entry in *Dictionary of American Biography* (New York: Scribner's, 1931) VII, 181, and J. Herman Schauinger, *William Gaston, Carolinian* (Milwaukee: Bruce Publishing Co., 1949).
19. The letter is reproduced in "Letter of Hamilton C. Jones the Elder," *North Carolina University Magazine* XXIII (April 1893): 212–220. Jones was still a tutor at the University of North Carolina when he wrote to Mitchell; this must have been a short stay in New Bern before he resumed his duties in Chapel Hill.
20. Hope Summerell Chamberlain, *This Was Home* (Chapel Hill: University of North Carolina Press, 1938), pp. 15–16. For detailed information about Salisbury and Rowan county, we have used also James S. Brawley, *The Rowan Story, 1753–1953: A Narrative History of Rowan County, North Carolina* (Salisbury, N.C.: Rowan Printing Co., 1953).
21. William Gaston to W. B. Meares, June 23, 1808, reproduced in *Raleigh News & Observer*, July 26, 1884.
22. Hamilton C. Jones to William Gaston, July 2, 1829. Manuscripts Department, University of North Carolina at Chapel Hill Library.
23. For accounts of Gold Hill, see Brent C. Glass, "King Midas and Old Rip: The Gold Hill Mining District of North Carolina." (Ph.D. diss., University of North Carolina at Chapel Hill, 1980); and Brawley, *The Rowan Story*.
24. Quoted in Schauinger, *William Gaston, Carolinian*, pp. 165–166.
25. U.S. census records for Rowan county, North Carolina, for 1840, 1850, 1860.
26. John Hill Wheeler, *Historical Sketch of North Carolina* (Baltimore: Regional Publishing Co., 1964), p. 395, and *Reminiscences and Memoirs of North Carolina and Eminent North Carolinians*, p. 407, quoted in Franklin J. Meine's unpublished manuscript on Jones, Rare Book and Special Collections Library, University of Illinois at Urbana-Champaign Library.
27. "Letter of Hamilton C. Jones the Elder," edited by Battle, p. 215.
28. *Carolina Watchman*, January 25, 1883, p. 2.
29. From an unpublished manuscript on Hamilton C. Jones by Franklin J. Meine, Rare Book and Special Collections Library, University of Illinois at UrbanaChampaign Library.
30. Cecil D. Eby, Jr., *"Porte Crayon": The Life of David Hunter Strother* (Chapel Hill: University of North Carolina Press, 1960), p. 92; Porte Crayon, "North Carolina Illustrated," *Harper's New Monthly Magazine* XV (August 1857): 289–300. For an excellent summary of this episode, see Walser, "Ham Jones: Southern Folk Humorist," p. 315.
31. In addition to the accounts of Col. Jones's wartime adventures published

in the *Watchman*, we have also used his biographical sketch in Samuel A. Ashe's *Biographical History of North Carolina* (Greensboro, N.C.: Charles L. Van Noppen, 1908).

32. Brawley, *The Rowan Story*, pp. 196–198.
33. Ibid., p. 200.

A NOTE ON THE TEXT

Walter Blair and Raven I. McDavid, Jr., in their useful and entertaining book *The Mirth of a Nation: America's Great Dialect Humor* (Minneapolis: University of Minnesota Press, 1983), attempted to make nineteenth-century humor (including Ham Jones's "Cousin Sally Dilliard") more accessible to the reading public by modernizing "paragraphing, capitalization, and punctuation" and normalizing "eccentric but meaningless, unfunny, or confusing spellings." Since Ham Jones's texts pose no major problems, we are not following the example of Blair and McDavid. We are presenting the stories as they were published for a nineteenth-century audience, leaving intact the colorful peculiarities of style, which help the reader understand the provincial culture of Jones's North Carolina at that time.

In every case, we are using the first printed version of a story or sketch. There are slight variations in later printings, but we have no evidence that Jones sanctioned those minor changes. We have silently corrected a few obvious typographical errors. We provide, at the end of the volume, a glossary of words and terms and identifications of some of the historical persons named in the stories. An asterisk indicates that the word, expression, or name is to be found in the glossary.

A NOTE ON THE ARRANGEMENT
OF MATERIALS

We have divided the stories in this anthology into four sections. The first contains the eight stories known to have been written by Jones.

The second section contains a selection from his short "Omnibus" contributions to his newspaper, the *Carolina Watchman*, and two miscellaneous items, one poem signed by Jones and an unsigned account of a dog poisoning probably written by Jones.

The third section contains four pieces probably written by Ham Jones. All four items appeared unsigned in the *Carolina Watchman*. His manuscripts have not survived, and it is not possible for us to establish his authorship conclusively, but they have the earmarks of his known work.

The fourth section presents five stories republished in the *Carolina Watchman*. As editor of a newspaper, Ham Jones received many journals and newspapers on exchange, and he often reprinted humorous stories from them. We believe these reprinted stories give an important indication of his taste in humor.

We provide brief introductions for each of the four sections, and we conclude with a glossary. We hope to do for Ham Jones what John Q. Anderson did for Dr. Henry Clay Lewis in *Louisiana Swamp Doctor*: rescue from oblivion a Southern humorist.

ACKNOWLEDGMENTS

We are indebted to Richard Walser; we have profited greatly from his books and articles, especially his "Ham Jones: Southern Folk Humorist," which appeared in the October–December 1965 issue of the *Journal of American Folklore*.

We also wish to acknowledge the assistance we have received from the librarians of the Rare Book and Special Collections Library of the University of Illinois at Urbana-Champaign (where the Franklin J. Meine Collection is housed); the staff of the North Carolina State Archives in Raleigh; librarians at the University of North Carolina at Chapel Hill, especially Ms. Alice R. Cotten; and Ms. Shirley Hoffman of the Rowan Public Library in Salisbury. The library of East Carolina University provided us, through interlibrary loan, with microfilm copies of the *Carolina Watchman*.

Hamilton C. Jones' great-grandson, William Erwin Jones, has also assisted us in many ways.

PART ONE

Stories and Sketches
by Ham Jones

INTRODUCTION

Hamilton C. Jones's first published story, "Cousin Sally Dilliard" (in reprints "Dilliard" was often spelled "Dillard"), originally appeared in *Atkinson's Saturday Evening Post* on August 6, 1831. It was an immediate success. Its humor comes through easily when read, and it is a story that can be told with great comic effect. "Cousin Sally Dilliard" is one of the earliest printed examples of "Southern and Southwestern humor," appearing four years before Longstreet's famous *Georgia Scenes*. Published at a time when American writing was moralistic, it avoided a moral tag, as much Southern and Southwestern humor in later periods was to do also.

The setting of the story is rural North Carolina; there had been a fight at Captain Rice's "treat," no doubt because of the large amount of corn liquor available at the entertainment. The characters in the story include a pompous young lawyer whose language is highly inflated and a drunken witness who uses the rural dialect and who seemingly knows that his rambling testimony was an act of subornation. The humor derives from the characters, their language, the setting, the witness's constant repetition of irrelevant details, all leading up to his final and entirely nonsensical testimony: "And that's the height of what I know about it." Franklin J. Meine has rightly called it "one of the earliest and most widely-read of all the humorous stories."[1]

The source of the story is not known. There were many people named Rice in Rowan County, North Carolina, at that time. Hope Summerell Chamberlain in *This Was Home* says that Captain Rice, the "treat" giver in the story, was an acquaintance of her family. When he saw her mother's sketch of columns of a Greek temple he remarked: "Now I reckon that mought* be a plan of the new courthouse, ain't it?"² It is likely that Jones based his story on real people and a real happening in a Piedmont court.

After Jones's death, however, there was a charge that the story was of Virginia origin and was told in that state long before it was known in North Carolina. A writer for the *Carolina Watchman* (probably J. J. Bruner, editor of the paper, who had known Jones well) on January 25, 1883, responded that he had often heard the story discussed in Jones's presence and that Jones never denied authorship. The writer went on, "We think the foundation of the story was obtained in one of the courts of this part of North Carolina, Stokes or Surry, shortly after Mr. Jones entered into the practice of the law. It is entirely inconsistent with the well known character of Mr. Jones that he should have permitted his friends to believe for years that he was the author and take no pains to correct it, if indeed he was not the true author."³

The story was not destined to remain locked in the files of *Atkinson's Saturday Evening Post*. William T. Porter late in 1831 founded in New York a sporting magazine called *The Spirit of the Times*, appealing largely to Southern and Western sportsmen and with a pronounced aristocratic bias. As Norris W. Yates has shown in *William T. Porter and The Spirit of the Times*, the humor published in the magazine was written by journalists, lawyers, doctors, and planters who were, from their perspectives, attempting to depict frontier life and manners. The writers were generally amateurs, and many used pseudonyms or disguised their authorship, as Jones did when he signed his later stories "By the author of 'Cousin Sally Dilliard.' " *The Spirit* often reprinted material from other publications and on March 24, 1832, reproduced "Cousin Sally" with this prefatory note: "The following exquisite morceau has already appeared in a contemporary print; but we readily adopt the suggestion of a friend to treat our patrons with a re-publication of it. The fidelity of the copy will recommend it to many a reader, who has probably seen many originals, that might have sat for the portrait."[4]

Porter was so pleased with the story that he reprinted it on May 14, 1836, on May 18, 1844, and on November 21, 1857. In his *The Big Bear of Arkansas and Other Sketches* he printed the story with this note: "Who knows but this sketch may have suggested to Judge LONGSTREET his side-splitting 'Georgia Scenes?' "[5] Many other editors evidently shared Porter's enthusiasm for the story, for it was reprinted often in the press. And, of course, it was imitated. Richard Walser has summarized two of these imitations:

> In "The Sequel to 'Capt. Rice's Treat,' " reprinted from the Memphis *Appeal*, a North Carolinian settling in Arkansas is asked by a stranger for directions to John Smith's house. Instead of complying, he talks of everything except the directions, about which he keeps saying, ". . . if there is anything in this world I *do* know, it is the way to John Smith's." Finally the exasperated traveler curses and departs, thoroughly annoyed by the *"amplification."* In another imitation, "Cousin Sally Dillard Outdone," the scene is "Chatham during the session of the Circuit court," when the tiresome recitation by a witness finally concludes with the admission that he had not seen the stabbing, because, he says, "I want* thar."[6]

Ham Jones was long an admirer of *The Spirit of the Times.* The *Carolina Watchman* in 1833 carried advertisements for *The Spirit*, and on May 18 of that year Jones informed his readers that the sporting magazine was filled "with more life, humour, fashion and *bon gout* than any we get hold of, and though we on a short acquaintance discover inequality in its numbers, we are constrained to say the most indifferent is *very good.* We commend it to the gay and fashionable world, and to all who think it 'good to be merry and wise.' " Jones often reprinted *Spirit* stories and anecdotes in his newspaper and must have learned from the journal a great deal about humor and ways to write it.

The next story in this section, "The Lost Breeches," appeared in the *Carolina Watchman* on January 19, 1833. Jones goes to great length to identify the teller of this story, a Captain Kincannon, who had been a hero in the revolutionary war. Jones described Kincannon's peculiarities of speech and manner, and urged readers to keep those qualities in mind, for he planned to print other stories by Kincannon in the paper. Unfortunately those other stories, if they were written, have not survived; less than fifty percent of the issues of the *Watchman* for the years Jones edited it have been preserved. The story has many elements of the traditional folktale: the yokel who makes a fool of himself, is robbed by the charcoal workers, and learns a lesson. It is Kincannon who adds the moral tag, saying of the yokel: "He used afterwards to say, that he had learned more in that one day's trip than many find out in their whole lives; he had found out that he was a fool, and that home was the best place for him." The yokel, then, is treated at the end with sympathy, for after the indignity of having lost his breeches, he is able to recognize his own foolishness in the matter.

Jones's next humorous sketch in the section, "McAlpin's Trip to Charleston," was originally published in *The Spirit of the Times* on July 11, 1846, and then reprinted by Porter in *A Quarter Race in Kentucky and Other Sketches*. McAlpin was indeed a rustic (but not a fool), sent to the city to negotiate the purchase of a plot of land. The reader has considerable sympathy for McAlpin: when he asked directions from a Charleston dandy, his civil request was answered by *"Go to h—l, you fool!"* At Col. Lamar's home, he was greatly impressed by the furnishings and by the beauty of Mrs. Lamar, but he was unnerved when his attempt to carve the turkey ended in a horrible fiasco, causing him such great anguish that the next thing he remembered was being on the hearth "a-kicking." Jones goes beyond the usual tale of the country bumpkin in the city, and arouses the reader's sympathy for the cracker* who in his gaucherie creates havoc in aristocratic surroundings.

"Going to Muster in North Carolina" was published in *The Spirit of the Times* on July 18, 1846. In North Carolina at that time all free white males between the ages of eighteen and forty-five were members of the militia and required to report for muster at least two times a year. These musters were, as a social historian has reported, "ordinarily looked upon as a holiday and celebrated as such by heavy drinking, betting, fighting, and sports."[7] The story is being told by a politician friend of Ham Jones's, a friend recalling the day he went to his first muster. The young man watches an old man prepare for muster, but eventually the old man's wife forbids him to go, not wanting him to spend all his money, get drunk, and wallow in the dirt. The story is part social comment, and it is clear that Jones meant to hold up to scorn the institution of military training. As in many of Jones's sketches, the situation is comic, but the story is not.

"The Sandy Creek Literary Society," published in *The Spirit of the Times* on August 15, 1846, is one of Ham Jones's most entertaining stories. It, too, is a framework story told by Fred Thompson, a tavern keeper who lived near Salisbury. Thompson liked to tell stories about his ignorant neighbors, especially Squire Ben Primm, a man who always pronounced "o" as if it were "a"—thus *harse* for *horse*. The effect of this peculiarity is similar to Victor Borge's comic monologues with verbal punctuation. The story satirizes at length the pretensions of the Sandy Creek "literary" crackers—and their piety—for it is during Squire Primm's long prayer that Bill Jenkins plays his "stinging" practical joke.

"The Round Robin," drawing its form from the Declaration of Independence, was a comic attack on the food, drink, service, and accommodations of the taverns and inns of the time. Lawyers on the circuit were at the mercy of the innkeepers, and while the story has a satiric tone, it is also obvious that Jones intended it as an indictment of the appalling living conditions that travelers often found in taverns and inns. The story originally appeared in *The Spirit of the Times* on August 22, 1846.

"The Frenchman and His Menagerie," filled with the broken English of a Frenchman, appeared in *The Spirit of the Times* on March 16, 1850. Jones may well have been fond of dialogue in broken English (or fractured French) because of his long acquaintance with the Reverend Mr. Frontis, the Huguenot minister of the Salisbury Presbyterian Church. The Rev. Mr. Frontis's English was uncertain, and once he blessed a young couple after the marriage ceremony with these words: "May the Lord peekle you both."[8] The minister may also have provided some of the French sources for this violent tale.

Jones, a man with a classical education, makes some obvious references to events in Roman times. The setting is a menagerie confined within a tent, and the connections with the Roman circus are obvious: Bill Reaves and his friends are gladiatorlike as they face the mountain panther. Even unsophisticated readers of *The Spirit of the Times* had heard or read accounts of Romans casting Christians into the ring with man-eating lions and of the fights of gladiators. Jones, then, connects the action of his story with the barbarism and excesses of Roman circuses.

Jones also draws on several violent European traditions, and Robert Darnton's essay "Workers Revolt: The Great Cat Massacre of the Rue Saint-Severin" in *The Great Cat Massacre* provides us with additional clues about ways to approach this strange and difficult story. Darnton reproduces Contat's account of a cat massacre in Paris in the late 1730s. Badly treated printer apprentices revolted against their master, hung the favorite cat of their mistress, and killed all the other cats they could find. The apprentices in this original version were delighted by the disorder and at least twenty times in subsequent days they staged burlesque reenactments of the cat massacre. Darnton points out that "our own inability to get the joke is an indication of the distance that separates us from the workers of preindustrial Europe."[9]

Following Darnton, we need to ask what the ruffians in preindustrial Ashe County, North Carolina, were rebelling against. The answer: against two confidence men, one of whom was a Yankee, and against women. Jones does not allow the Yankee to speak, instead he calls upon the usual perception of the Yankee at that time: a shrewd, often unscrupulous man. By 1850 the Yankee of myth had been tarred with the brush of abolitionism, and the proslavery tide was growing throughout the South. Jones moves his Yankee trickster to the side and concentrates on the French confidence man; Jones suggests that the menagerie had once been more legitimate but that a cold winter had killed off many of the tropical animals. The owners had then filled out their show with animals readily available to them, and had misidentified some of them; for instance, the common mountain panther was presented as a tiger. The Frenchman has exquisite manners, but he is nevertheless a confidence man.

The rebellion against women as presented in the story would have been easily grasped in the nineteenth century. The North Carolina mountaineers in the mock trial and execution of the large cat were acting out part of their European heritage, for cats were connected with witchcraft and the female principle. It was still widely believed that witches could turn themselves into cats for those night sabbaths all could hear in the form of caterwauling at night. Citizens could protect themselves from the sorcery of cats by killing or maiming the cats. In folklore, cats also represented the female principle. Jones's ruffians lived in a male-dominated society that had contempt for many of the "civilizing" ways of women. The good times of the men were to be had at the military musters, at the races, at the taverns, on election days—all male-dominated occasions. During these festive times, the men escaped women, but the festivals lasted only a short time. The killing of the cat does suggest the deep animosity toward women in Southern culture.

Folklorists have pointed out the importance of ceremonial cycles that marked the calendars of early modern man, one of the most important of which was carnival time preceding Lent—a period of revelry, excesses, and real and symbolic violence. Though there was no carnival time as such in the Protestant South during the nineteenth century, there were events that called forth a carnival-like atmosphere: the military musters, horse racing days, weddings, and circuses. At all of these there was much drinking and fighting, and it was a time when order was subverted.

Jones makes it clear that his Bill Reaves gladiator types are capable of violence. They are sophisticated in their knowledge of wild animals and know that they are safe in offering to fight the mountain panther, because they know it has little fighting spirit. The fight, then, between the gladiators and the mountain panther is a sham, and the panther is defeated. Then the panther is forced to fight the monkey, with its humanlike qualities, but the small monkey is no match for the panther and is killed. In Roman times, the lion who killed the Christian was executioner, acting lawfully for the state. In the North Carolina mock trial of the panther, however, the executioner is found guilty. The humor is in wordplay: manslaughter-monkeyslaughter. The situation itself is not comic.

The story also draws upon the European custom of executing

animals found guilty of crimes. E. P. Evans in *The Criminal Persecution and Capital Punishment of Animals* collected a large number of examples of animals convicted and executed. For example, in 1394 a pig in France killed a child and ate of its flesh. The courts found the pig guilty of murder and ordered it executed. North Carolinian mountaineers were not long removed from their European heritage: they also believed in the ancient doctrine of an eye for an eye, a tooth for a tooth, and applied that belief in their own mock trial.

Hamilton Jones, that educated, worldly wise man, in writing about the human comedy in an event in Ashe County, North Carolina, allows us to compare the civilization of the mountaineers with that of Rome. He makes connections between the cruelties of a Roman circus and those within a menagerie tent in the nineteenth-century South, and he shows that ancient rituals continue, in only slightly modified form, in his own time. He also does not let the reader believe that justice will prevail. Instead, he has the ringleaders of the event charged with riot, but he carefully does not divulge the verdict of the court. It was certainly unlikely that an Ashe County court would convict local citizens who rioted against a Frenchman and a Yankee, confidence men who lost their entrance fees, their monkey, and their panther at the hands of ruffians who would not be conned. In this story Jones shows us the darkest side of Southern life—its suspicions of outsiders, its cruelty and sadism, and its lawlessness.[10]

Jones's last story in *The Spirit of the Times* appeared on August 23, 1851. In "Abel Hucks in a Tight Place" Jones moved from the violence of "The Frenchman and His Menagerie" to a rather quiet story presenting a rustic from Union County, North Carolina, and his reaction to unusual and improvised punishment. Abel Hucks is the teller of his own story in a letter to Porter, editor of *The Spirit*. Abel had suffered all his life from a sense of inadequacy—he was short of stature and poor. Apparently to compensate, he turned to moonshine. When he was a little drunk, he had a fight with a tall man. Abel was brought into court and sentenced to the stocks. Union County had only recently been organized, and its county seat, Monroe, did not yet have stocks, or even a jail. The sheriff improvised by putting Abel's legs through the rails of a fence. Abel was humiliated and asked Porter: "I want to know whether it is accordin' to the American Constitution, to put a fellers legs through a rail fence because they haven't got stocks in a new county?" Jones holds himself up to ridicule in the story; Abel writes that Jones was "that queer-looking feller." The magistrate in the story was Judge Battle, Jones's classmate at the University of North Carolina. We assume that Abel and the rail fence around the courthouse in Monroe both existed! The basic situation in the story is comic—real stocks would have been tolerable, but a rail fence was degrading. Abel has the reader's sympathy when he threatens to move to South Carolina and help make a constitution that forbids such indignity.

The way a story was told was clearly of interest to Ham Jones. In those stories with a narrator (particularly "The Lost Breeches" and "The Sandy Creek Literary Society") the narrator's manner of speaking—and in some cases his appearance—are highly important, the framework of the story adding yet another level of humor. Ham Jones liked to experiment with forms; he began his writing career with a work that was to become a classic—"Cousin Sally Dilliard"— told almost entirely in dialogue. A good storyteller, having read the account, could then improvise, work out speech patterns and facial expressions, and present his own version to listeners. At other times (as in "The Frenchman and His Menagerie" and "McAlpin's Trip to Charleston") Jones has an omniscient observer tell the story; these stories read well, but they, too, could easily be adapted for oral telling. "Abel Hucks in a Tight Place" is in the form of a letter to the editor of *The Spirit of the Times*, and Jones makes good comic use of Abel's spellings—and his world view. "The Round Robin" uses the form of the Declaration of Independence. Part of the humor derives from the disparity between British iniquities and bad food and lodging in Southern inns.

A man of property and position, Hamilton C. Jones used his humor to reflect the life he saw around him. He had a good ear for the language of the people, and he used that talent well in the stories he told of his fellow Tar Heels. These stories used stereotypes of the French, Yankees, women, blacks, innkeepers, politicians, poor whites, and others. He was conservative in his own political and social views, but he was aware of and understood the ignorance and violence of the people in whose midst he lived, and he almost always avoided moralizing. His works seem to be based on real people and real events, and the stereotypes were present in the folk material he reworked. As Walser has noted, many of Ham Jones's most successful stories are "anecdotes of the folk which he had listened to and had decided to record for publication."[11] His surviving sketches, stories, poems, and anecdotes do not make up a large body of work, but they capture the vitality of his region in the three decades before the Civil War. In his stories he followed the stated object of *The Spirit of the Times*: "To paint 'life as it is,' without the artificial embellishments of romance. . . . For it is certainly no more improper to record the acts of men than to promulgate them morally to the world."[12]

NOTES

1. Norris W. Yates, *William T. Porter and The Spirit of the Times* (Baton Rouge: LSU Press, 1957), p. 105.
2. Hope S. Chamberlain, *This Was Home* (Chapel Hill: University of North Carolina Press, 1938), p. 89.
3. *Carolina Watchman*, January 25, 1883, p. 2. In *The Big Bear of Arkansas* (1845) William T. Porter wrote that "Cousin Sally Dilliard" "is understood to have been written by Hamilton C. Jones," but Jones's authorship of that story was not generally known to the American public.
4. *The Spirit of the Times*, March 24, 1832, p. 2.
5. Porter, *The Big Bear of Arkansas*, p. 178.
6. Richard Walser, "Ham Jones: Southern Folk Humorist," *Journal of American Folklore* 78 (October-December 1965):297.
7. Guion Griffis Johnson, *Ante-Bellum North Carolina: A Social History* (Chapel Hill: University of North Carolina Press, 1937), p. 102.
8. Chamberlain, *This Was Home*, p. 36.
9. Robert Darnton, *The Great Cat Massacre, and Other Episodes in French Cultural History* (New York: Basic Books, 1984), pp. 77–78.
10. See Stith Thompson, *Motif-Index of Folk-Literature*, (Bloomington: Indiana University Press, 1966), B–272.2 for "Animal tried for crime" and B–275.1 for "Animal executed for crime." For an account of cat torturing in eighteenth-century France, see Robert Darnton, *The Great Cat Massacre, and Other Episodes in French Cultural History*. See also E. P. Evans, *The*

Criminal Prosecution and Capital Punishment of Animals (London: Heinemann, 1906).

11. Walser, p. 315.

12. From a prospectus for *The Spirit of the Times* published in the *Carolina Watchman*, March 16, 1833, p. 4.

Communicated for the Saturday Evening Post.

COUSIN SALLY DILLIARD.

Scene—A Court of Justice, in No. Ca.

A beardless disciple of Themis* rises, and thus addresses the court:—May it please your Worships, and you, Gentlemen of the Jury, since it has been my fortune (good or bad I will not say) to exercise myself in legal disquisitions, it has never before befallen me to be obliged to denounce a breach of the peace so enormous and transcending as the one now claiming your attention. A more barbarous, direful, marked and malicious assault—a more wilful, violent, dangerous and murderous battery, and finally, a more diabolical breach of the peace has seldom happened in a civilized country, and I dare say it has seldom been your duty to pass upon one so shocking to benevolent feeling as this, which took place over at Captain Rice's, in this county, but you will hear from the witnesses. The witnesses being sworn, two or three were examined and deposed—one, that he heard the noise, but did'nt see the fight—another, that he saw the row, but don't know who struck first—and a third, that he was very drunk, and could'nt say much about the scrimmage.

Lawyer Chops.—I am sorry, gentlemen, to have occupied so much of your time with the stupidity of the witnesses examined. It arose, gentlemen, altogether from misapprehension on my part. Had I known, as I now do, that I had a witness in attendance, who was well acquainted with all the circumstances of the case, and who was able to make himself clearly and intelligibly understood by the court and jury, I should not so long have trespassed on your time and patience. Come forward, Mr. Harris, and be sworn.

So forward comes the witness, a fat, chuffy* looking man, a *"leetle" corned,* and took his corporal oath with an air.

Chops. Mr. Harris, we wish you to tell all about the riot that happened the other day at Captain Rice's, and as a good deal of time has been already wasted in circumlocution, we wish you to be as compendious and at the same time as explicit as possible.

Harris. "Edzactly,"—giving the lawyer a knowing wink, at the same time clearing his throat—Captain Rice, he gin a treat,* and cousin Sally Dilliard, she came over to our house and axed me if my wife, she mought'nt* go—I told cousin Sally Dilliard that my wife was poorly, being as how she had a touch of the Rheumatics in the hip, and the big swamp was in the road, and the big swamp was up, for there had been a heap of rain lately; but howsomever as it was she, cousin Sally Dilliard, my wife, she mought go.—Well, cousin Sally Dilliard than axed me if Mose, he mought'nt go. I told cousin Sally Dilliard that Mose, he was the foreman of the crop, and the crop was smartly in the grass; but howsomever as it was she, cousin Sally Dilliard, Mose, he mout go.

Chops. In the name of common sense, Mr. Harris, what do you mean by this rigmarole.

Witness. Captain Rice, he gin a treat, and cousin Sally Dilliard, she came over to our house and axed me if my wife, she mougt'nt go. I told cousin Sally Dilliard—

Chops. Stop, sir, if you please; we don't want to hear any thing about cousin Sally Dilliard and your wife—tell us about the fight at Rice's.

Witness. Well, I will, sir, if you will let me.

Chops. Well, sir, go on.

Witness. Well, Captain Rice, he gin a treat, and cousin Sally Dilliard, she came over to our house [and] axed me if my wife, she mougt'nt go—

Chops. There it is again,—witness, I say, witness, please to stop.

Witness. Well, sir, what as you want?

Chops. We want to know about the fight, and you must not proceed in this impertinent story—do you know any thing about the matter before the Court?

Witness. To be sure I do.

Chops. Will you go on and tell it, and nothing else?

Witness. Well, Captain Rice, he gin a treat—

Chops. This is intolerable! May it please the Court—I move that this witness be committed for a contempt,—he seems to me to be trifling with the court.

Court. Witness, you are now before a Court of Justice, and unless you behave yourself in a more becoming manner, you will be sent to jail; so begin and tell what you know about the fight at Captain Rice's.

Witness, (alarmed.) Well, gentlemen, Captain Rice, he gin a treat, and cousin Sally Dilliard—

Chops. I hope that this witness may be ordered into custody.

Court. (after deliberating.) Mr. Attorney, the Court is of opinion that we may save time by telling the witness to go on in his own way.—Proceed, Mr. Harris, with your story, but stick to the point.

Witness. Yes, gentlemen: well, Captain Rice, he gin a treat, and cousin Sally Dilliard, she came over to our house, and axed me if my wife, she mougt'nt go. I told cousin Sally Dilliard that my wife was poorly, being as how she had the Rheumatics in the hip, and the big swamp was in the road, and the big swamp was up; but howsomever, as it was she, cousin Sally Dilliard, my wife, she mougt go. Well, Cousin Sally Dilliard then axed me if Mose, he mougt'nt go. I told cousin Sally Dilliard as how Mose, he was the foreman of the crop, and the crop was smartly in the grass; but howsomever, as it was she, cousin Sally Dilliard, Mose, he mougt go. So on they goes together, Mose, my wife, and cousin Sally Dilliard, and they comes to the big swamp, and the big swamp was up, as I was telling you; but being as how there was a log across the big swamp, cousin Sally Dilliard and Mose, like genteel folks, they walks the log, but my wife, like a d—d fool, hoists up her petticoats and waded, and, gentlemen, that's the height of what I know about it.

Atkinson's Saturday Evening Post, August 6, 1831, p. [4].

CAPT. KINCANNON—OF SURRY

Few persons in Stokes and Surry have not heard of old Capt. Kincannon of Surry. He was remarkable for an uncommonly strong mind—for his strict integrity—for evenness of temper, and for a certain quaint humor, that was inimitable. His manner was unpretending and extremely dry. We have seen him have a crowd of listeners fairly convulsed with laughter, while his own hard features remained as rigid as the rock on the Pilot [a mountain in North Carolina], that overlooked his residence. The old Gentleman had become somewhat paralytic in his latter days, and the tremulousness of his speech and gestures, had an effect to heighten the contrast between his matter and the manner of his conversing. Before we proceed further in our details concerning this favorite of our boyhood, and indeed, of our after life, we must premise that he was a Captain in the battle of King's Mountain, and was known to have acted with great bravery in that and on other occasions in the Revolutionary War. We have often heard him declare that the charge of cowardice brought against Col. Campbell,* after his death, was not true. He on all occasions, when called on, stated his opportunities of knowing the facts, and his various reasons for believing that the charge was untrue. The Editor of this paper, who was very familiarly acquainted with Capt. Kincannon, proposed to write out the circumstances and let them go to the world, while the country was still agitated, but he refused. He said he was too obscure to obtrude his name on the public—that he never had had a dispute on politics or any thing of any kind either public or private, that he did not wish in the evening of his days to be involved in an angry conflict. He has been dead several years, say four or five—and we wish it could be emblazoned on a more enduring page that Captain Kincannon combined more of the useful, the wise, the pleasant and innocent than any man we ever knew; he was truly *"as wise as a serpent and as harmless as a dove."*

We give the above sketch of Captain Andrew Kincannon, because we intend now and then to give some of his diverting stories, and unless you keep the man in your mind's eye, and his manner, you will lose one half of the relish. We wish our readers, therefore, to preserve this little notice, and hereafter, when we detail any thing as coming from him, we want you to advert to this description. He was a tall, rawboned man, remarkably stout, and was scarcely ever known to be sick, except the slight attack of paralysis, which we have mentioned. His face was of the severest Scotch mould, long, with high cheek bones, a keen grey eye, large eyebrows, and an immense mouth. To look at him, you would think him a perfect Cynic Philosopher, yet he was a lamb in gentleness and humanity. The following story is on his authority and is undoubtedly true.

THE LOST BREECHES

One evening, said Capt. K., two men rode up to my house, which was about a mile from the main Hollow Road. The foremost one was a round, consequential looking man on a fat horse, and rode with his legs established in a firm position at a considerable angle with his body.—"Halloo, sir! can I get to stay with you tonight?" "Yes sir," said I. I never turn off any one that stumbles upon my out of the way house. "If you are willing to put up with such things as we can afford, you are welcome to stay." "Well, but" says the pragmatical looking traveller, "what's the chance? What can you give us?" "Why," says the Captain, "it's rather a poor chance I doubt." "Is it," says the fellow, and began to look inquisitively about, and doubtingly to his companion, as to know what he thought of going further. His companion answered his enquiry by throwing both legs on the same side of his horse, and letting go the rein of his bridle, as much as to say, I'll risk it at all events. "But then," said the spokesman, "may be, you can let us have something tolerable." "Yes," said the Captain, "we can let you have food for your horses, and meat and bread for yourselves at least"—"Well, can you let us have a fried chicken?" "Yes," said the old gentleman. "Why, criminy," says the traveller, "pretty tolerable chance—Any biscuits, Landlord?" "Yes" said the Captain, "*and butter.*" "Butter too," exclaimed the stranger—"why it's not so poor a chance after all—Well, how about coffee?" "Coffee," said the old man—"Aye," said he, "and that that's good," (by this time he had smoked the fellow to be an upstart,) "and I can tell you another thing," said he, "and that's an important one—you can have *sugar too.*" "Sugar too," exclaimed the fellow, "that's a d—d good chance—take my horse sir, I'll stay with you." Accordingly the horses were taken, and the Travellers enstalled into the best room in the house, and as the round man we are speaking of seemed very choice, and knowing, the cookwench did her very best, and an uncommonly good supper was provided. I endured a good deal of loquacity and presumption until bed time, said the Captain—was contradicted in matters where my senses were my informants—heard much of my entertainer's wealth, his manner of churning, of threshing, of plowing, of bringing up his children, managing his family, &c., &c. He spoke of things happening in Guilford county, as if he thought it lay beyond the Atlantic—strange sights, scenes, battles, murders, &c., &c. At length, his companion perceiving, I suppose, that I was not so much surprised at these wonderful narrations, as to forget that there was such a thing as sleep, at length, after several propositions to that effect, he got a motion towards going to bed. "Well, stranger," said he, "we intend to be off before day, so we will pay you before we go to bed; what do I owe you sir?" (rattling the change in his breeches pocket.) "Nothing at all sir," replied Capt. K. "Nothing at all?" repeated the other. "Why, that's strange—we have put you to a good deal of trouble, and I insist on paying you *half price* at least." I positively refused several times to take any thing—every time he came over the expression, that he had put me to a *heap of trouble.* I told him that he had put me to more inconvenience to get rid of his importunities than any thing else. So if he would go to bed and say no more about his money that we would quit even: This seemed to stump him somewhat: He said then, that he would give it to my negro; "you may give him as much as you please," said I, and at length got rid of him. I thought but little of Mr.—, or of his wealth or his wife, or his churning or of any thing that was his, they were off by times in the morning; and I should have never thought of him again but for what afterwards occurred. About nine the next day, I had gone out from home some miles to look after some trifling fellows whom I had employed to cut coalwood,* the spot was one of the most sequestered and difficult to approach of any in that mountainous region. When I came in sight of the coaling ground, I looked around for my workmen, but they were not to be seen or heard; I was not much surprised at this, for they had often treated me in that way; but this being their sober week, viz: they being out of means to buy liquor with, I had expected rather better of them. I was loitering about the ground, observing their previous days work, when of a sudden, I came right upon a man screwed up in one corner of an old log camp, whom to my surprise, I recognized as my loquacious Guest of the evening before. He looked like a man taken in a criminal act. I expressed my astonishment at his being there, and began to hint my suspicions—when he came out at once. "No, my good sir," said he, "you must not believe thus of me; I am a fool, and while running over my folly in yonder's cold log cabin, I came to the conclusion, that I was a d——d fool; but I am no rogue, to tell the truth, I never was this far from home before in my life; when I started to travel to Tennessee, my wife made me a pair of drawers—the first I ever had on in my life. I went to bed with them on last night—this morning, starting before light, I feeling as warm as usual with my drawers on, never once thought of my breeches—so I rode off and left them, and never thought of them till I had got ten miles off. Of course, I turned back for them, for all my money is in the pocket of them; but my companion went on. I felt so much ashamed to go *back for my breeches* to a house where I had put on so many airs of a gentleman, that I resolved to circle through the woods until I could find some one to go after them, and after a pretty difficult ride through the bushes and mountain knobs, I found your wood cutters, whom I have hired to go after my breeches." "Did you tell them there was money in them," said I—"I did" said he; well, I told him it was a bad chance to get either breeches or money. I saw him eye me when I used the word chance. We soon hurried to my house, but the prize was gone—the messengers had so far promptly done their errand, but where they were then to be found was a matter of difficulty. I had the Guilford gentleman stowed away in a pair of my pantaloons, in which he could have carried his whole person, and we took the road to the nearest retail shop; but to the enquiry after a pair of stray breeches, which the Sansculotte Gentleman put, they answered that they knew nothing. We then hastened to another and another—and to the same enquiry after a pair of stray breeches, the same answer was given; the fact was, that my rascally cutters not having chanced to so much money perhaps ever before, thought best to make out of the neighborhood. And the poor gentleman humbled to death and mortified, took the road homewards, and never ventured upon his travels again. He used afterwards to say, that he had learned more in that one day's trip than many find out in their whole lives; he had found out that he was a fool, and that home was the best place for him.

Carolina Watchman, January 19, 1833, p.1.

McALPIN'S TRIP TO CHARLESTON

Written for the "Spirit of the Times" by the author of
"Cousin Sally Dilliard."

In the country of Robeson, in the State of North Carolina, there lived in times past a man by the name of BROOKS who kept a grocery for a number of years, and so had acquired most of the land around him. This was mostly pine barrens of small value, but nevertheless Brooks was looked up to as a great landholder and big man in the neighborhood. There was one tract, however, belonging to one Col. LAMAR, who lived in Charleston, that *"jammed in upon him so strong,"* and being withal better in quality than the average of his own domain, that Brooks had long wished to add it to his other broad acres. Accordingly he looked around him and employed, as he expressed it, "the smartest man in the neighborhood," to wit, one ANGUS McALPIN, to go to Charleston and negociate with Col. Lamar for the purchase of this also. Being provided pretty well with bread, meat, and a bottle of *paleface,** which were stowed away in a pair of leather saddle bags, and like all other great *Plenipotentiaries,* being provided with suitable instructions, Mac mounted a piney-wood-stacky* (named Rasum) and hied him off to Charleston. The road was rather longer than Brooks had supposed, or his agent was less expeditious, or some bad luck had happened to him, or something was the matter that Angus did not get back until long after the day had transpired, which was fixed on for his return. Brooks in the meantime had got himself into a very fury of impatience. He kept his eyes fixed on the Charleston road—he was crusty towards his customers—harsh towards his wife and children, and scarcely eat or slept for several days and nights, for he had set his whole soul upon buying the Lamar land. One day, however, Angus was descried slowly and sadly wending his way up the long stretch of sandy road that made up to the grocery. Brooks went out to meet him, and, without further ceremony, he accosted him.

"Well, Mac, have you got the land?"

The agent, in whose face was any thing but sunshine, replied somewhat gruffly that "he might let a body get down from his horse before he put at him with questions of business."

But Brooks was in a fever of anxiety and repeated the question—"Did you get it?"

"Shaw,* now, Brooks, don't press upon a body in this uncivil way. It is a long story and I must have time."

Brooks still urged and Mac still parried the question till they got into the house.

"Now, surely," thought Brooks, "he will tell me." But Mac was not quite ready.

"Brooks," says he, "have you any thing to drink?"

"To be sure I have," said the other, and immediately had some of his best forth-coming. Having moistened his clay, Mac took a seat and his employer another. Mac gave a preliminary hem! He then turned suddenly around to Brooks, looked him straight in the eyes, and slapped him on the thigh—

"Brooks," says he, "was you ever in Charleston?"

"Why, you know I never was," replied the other.

"Well, then, Brooks," says the agent, "you ought to go there. The greatest place upon the face of the earth! They've got houses there on both sides of the road for five miles at a stretch, and d—n the horse-track the whole way through! Brooks, I think I met five thousand people in a minute, and not a chap would look at me. They have got houses there on wheels. Brooks! I saw one with six horses hitched to it, and a big driver with a long whip going it like a whirl-wind. I followed it down the road for a mile and half, and when it stopt I looked and what do you think there was? nothing in it but one little woman sitting up in one corner. Well, Brooks, I turned back up the road, and as I was riding along I sees a fancy looking chap with long curly hair hanging down his back, and his boots as shiney as the face of an up-country nigger! I called him into the middle of the road and asked him a civil question—and a civil question, you know, Brooks, calls for a civil answer all over the world. I says, says I, 'Stranger, can you tell me where Col. Lamar lives?' and what do you think was his answer—'*Go to h—l, you fool*!!'

"Well, Brooks, I knocks along up and down and about, until at last I finds out where Col. Lamar lived. I gets down and bangs away at the door. Presently the door was opened by as pretty, fine-spoken, well dressed a woman as ever you seed in your born days, Brooks. *Silks! Silks thar* every day, Brooks! Says I, 'Mrs Lamar, I presume, Madam,' says I. 'I am Mrs. Lamar, Sir.' 'Well, Madam,' says I, 'I have come all the way from North Carolina to see Colonel Lamar—to see about buying a tract of land from him that's up in our parts?' Then, she says, 'Col. Lamar has rode out in the country, but will be back shortly. Come in, Sir, and wait a while. I've no doubt the Colonel will soon return,' and she had a smile upon that pretty face of her's that reminded a body of a Spring morning. Well, Brooks, I hitched my horse to a brass thing on the door, and walked in. Well, when I got in I sees the floor all covered over with the nicest looking thing! nicer than any patched-worked bedquilt you ever seed in your life, Brooks. I was trying to edge along around it, but presently I sees a big nigger come stepping right over it. Thinks I if that nigger can go it I can go it, too! So right over it I goes and takes my seat right before a picture which at first I thought was a little man looking in at a window. Well, Brooks, there I sot waiting and waiting for Col. Lamar, and *at* last—he didn't come, but they began to bring in dinner. Thinks I to myself, here's a scrape. But I made up my mind to tell her, if she axed me to eat—to tell her with a genteel bow that I *had no occasion to eat*. But, Brooks, she didn't ax me to eat—she axed me if I'd be so good as to carve that turkey for her, and she did it with one of them lovely smiles that makes the cold streaks run down the small of a felles's back. 'Certainly, Madam,' says I, and I walks up to the table—there was on one side of the turkey a great big knife as big as a bowie knife, and a fork with a trigger to it on the other side. Well, I falls to work, and in the first *e*-fort I slashed the gravy about two yards over the whitest table cloth you ever seed in your life, Brooks! Well! I felt the hot steam begin to gather about my cheeks and eyes. But I'm not a man to back out for trifles, so I makes another *e*-fort and the darned thing took a flight and lit right in Mrs. Lamar's lap! Well, you see, Brooks, then I was taken with a blindness, and the next thing I remember I was upon the *hath** a-kicking. Well, by this time I began to think of navigating. So I goes out and mounts Rasum, and cuts for North Carolina! Now, Brooks, you don't blame me! Do you?"

The Spirit of the Times, July 11, 1846, p. 234.

GOING TO MUSTER IN NORTH CAROLINA

Written for the "Spirit of the Times" by the author of "Cousin Sally Dilliard."

JOHN S. GUTHRIE, Esq., of Chatham, long a member of the Legislature, was distinguished for his good sense, fine wit, and occasionally some of the most extraordinary bursts of eloquence. Our various passages (his and mine) have been too frequent and too notorious for me to get into print, and not he also. The fact is, if there was any painter on earth who could have apprehended the expression of John's face when he was in the proper vein—that broad, kind, habitual smile, the quizzical leer of that impatient grey eye, and above all, the longitudinal expansion of that mouth, with its peculiar curves and angles, I would have the picture for my frontispiece. Nothing could be more proper, either as a mark of my regard for the bearer of that face, or as a pre-exponent of the happy contents of these pages, their innocence and lightheartedness. But I have not set down to write the biography of John Guthrie, only to narrate an incident which he used himself to tell with inimitable glee.

He says that when he arrived at the age of eighteen, he was put upon the muster roll, and duly warned by the orderly of the company to appear on next Saturday morning at the usual parade ground, equipped according to law. John says that he knew well enough that he was eighteen years old, but the thought of bearing arms in the service of his country had never once crossed his brain; but when the idea was brought home to him by the summons of the subordinate of Captain DIDDLER, he says he did not know what he should do—so near being a man! So he went and whipped a big boy that had always kept him under, and took a dose of medicine for fear he should grow too fast!

Well, Saturday at length came, and off he starts, after an early breakfast, towards the glorious spot where he was to "shoulder arms," for the first time in his life, as a sure-enough soldier, and if he had not been stopped, he would have been at the muster-ground an hour at least before any one else. But as he was passing by old Mr. EMERSON's, he was hailed by that worthy to know where he was going? He quickly made known his destination, when the old man told him to come in and wait a while, for that he was going that way himself. John says he paused to consider what he should do; it looked like checking him in the dawn of his career to glory, but the old fellow insisted, and in he went. He sat for a while, and watched the slow and deliberate preparations of his proposed companion, and he thought he should have dropped down with impatience, but still the old man pursued the "even tenor of his way." He went to the kitchen, and got a tin cup of hot water;—he then took out a rusty razor, and strapped—strapped—strapped it, until—until he could have seen it drawn across the old chap's weasand.* He then quietly lathered his face, and then tugged and grinned, and relathered and tugged away again. He thought at length, by way of relief, of taking a conversation with the old lady, who was sitting by, knitting; but here comes the crisis of our story—old Mrs. Emerson was obviously in no very serene condition of temper, and his reception in this quarter was anything but entertaining.

"Mrs. Emerson," says he, "how do you come on raising chickens this year?"

"I don't know," replied she, in a quick, barking kind of voice.

Falls short, thinks John, but after sitting a while, he resolves to try her again—

"Mrs. Emerson, how do the girls come on getting sweethearts?"

"I don't know! I reckon you know as much about that as I do," says she.

He turned and discovered that there was a pent up storm in her face—her knitting needles were urged together with such emphasis that they sounded like castanets, and as she tossed the thread over the busy points, she had the air of throwing off her indignation from her fore-fingers. John then turned to notice the old man.

Having performed the operations of scraping and scouring he moved to a large chest, and taking out a shirt, pantaloons, waist-coat, and stockings, he proceeded towards the door of an adjacent room, with his clothes in his hand; but just about the time he had accomplished half that distance, Mrs. Emerson boiled over.

"Old man!" said she, straightening herself up and pointing with a long skinny finger right at him; the old fellow stopped, and made a sort of half face to the right. "Old man! Now you are going to that nasty muster, and there you'll get drunk and spend all your money; and you'll wallow in the dirt, and I shall have your clothes to wash. You *shan't go*!! YOU RALLY SHANT GO!!!"

"Well, old woman," says he, "there was no use in making such a terrible to do about it, for I had partly gin it out any how!"

John said he didn't wait for any excuse from the old man, but went forward and got to muster in full time.

The above was written before the death of Mr. Guthrie, which will account for the lightness as well as the scantiness of this notice.

The Spirit of the Times, July 18, 1846, p. 247.

THE SANDY CREEK LITERARY SOCIETY

By the author of "Cousin Sally Dilliard."

Mr. P.*—Some few years ago there lived a very facetious man on the road leading from Salisbury (North Carolina) to Salem; his name was FRED. THOMPSON. He kept an excellent house of entertainment and used to tell some good stories upon his ignorant neighbors. He had a spite towards his neighbor 'Squire BEN PRIMM, whom he delighted to take off—and to those who knew Ben (as I did), the humor was irresistible. The Squire was a small man, with a thin face, small mouth, straight nose, and dark projecting eyes. He was a man of pretty good sense, but he spoiled it all by the largeness of his pretensions, and by a most ridiculous mannerism. He was very fond of talking, and always delivered his words as if he was making a *set talk* or harangue. He held his head perfectly still, his eyes fixed to a point right before him, and every feature in his face, except his lips, seemed as if they had been cast on marble. His voice was pitched to a particular key, and he never so far deviated from the line of strict propriety as to fall below or rise above that pitch. His words were delivered as if they had been weighed and measured, and every syllable of every word, was as distinctly audible as the ticking of a clock in a bed room. He was what you would call a monstrous *precise* and *knowing* little man; talked a great deal about

---

61

"vartue" and "marality," and the blinding effects of ig-no-rance and su-per-sti-ti-on.

From the judicial exercise, incident to the office of Justice of the Peace, he had acquired a fondness for the use of law slang, particularly for the word "aforesaid." And when I have added that Ben always pronounced an O as if it were an A, thus—*"harse"* for *"horse,"* "Thampson" for "Thompson," &c, I have given you the outline of a character which your own fancy will fill up as our story proceeds.

I have described Ben pretty nearly as he really was; but Thompson used to exaggerate these ridiculous points very much, and would illustrate them by many comic stories. I will endeavor to give you one of them for the "Spirit of the Times," to wit: his account of

THE SANDY CREEK LITERARY SOCIETY.

Our friend 'Squire Ben, *"aforesaid,"* had lectured and electioneered until he had raised, by subscription, a small sum of money, and the contributors, according to previous notice, duly given, had collected together at Sandy Creek meeting house, to take measures for investing the fund on hand in books. Sherwood, as being by far the most knowing man in the neighborhood, was, as a matter of course, appointed Pres-i-dent, and P——— S——— was appointed Secretary. Being thus organized, Ben arose, and making one or two preliminary hems, proceeded thus—

"Friends and fellow members of the Sandy Creek Literary Society—I thank you for the *annor* you have done me by electing me to this *annorable* office, and all I can say further on that *taupic* is, to pledge my *annor* to you that I will faithfully *endeevor* to do my duty. We have met here, my friends, in arder to pravide the means to fartify our minds against ignarance and preju-*dice*: it is a lardable undertaking, and we hope will promote *vartue* and *marality* amang the rising generation—far I am bold to say, that nothing is better calculated to fartify the human mind than ancient and madern history. Will some of the society be so good as to begin the namination of the books? and I will put it to vote whether the aforesaid book shall pass or not. But I will suggest that none but *ancient* and *madern history* will be approved of. As to *navels*, I suppose that no gentleman would keep them about his house—far they are very detrimental to the marals of the rising generation, and very destructive to *vartue* in general; so I would, as aforesaid, advise against any prapasition to buy a navel. Will some of you begin the business by naminating a book?" [A pause, but no reply.]

Prest.—My friends, I hope some one of you will begin the work aforesaid. [No answer.]

The fact is, there was scarce one among them who had ever read a book, and it was a right serious requirement that their president was making.

Prest.—Well! if no one else will name a book, I will do so myself—I nominate the BIBLE, for it is the best ancient and *madern* history that ever was yet printed. All you who are in favor of the Bible say "aye"—they that are agin the Bible say "no." It is carried—Mr. Secretary, record that vote.

The Secretary wrote down BYBEL.

Prest.—Well, now, my friends, I have set you an example, I hope you will go on. [Pause.] Come, Mr. HELMSTETTER, name some book, as aforesaid.

The individual thus called out was a very ignorant man, particularly of letters. But as the eyes of all were upon him, he thought he would make a pass, at all events.

"I—I—name *Man Preceptor*,"* said he, very quick, and down he sat.

Prest.—Any ancient or modern history, as aforesaid, will be approved of, I presume.

The vote was taken, and passed in the affirmative—*unanimously*.

The Secretary proceeded to record that vote, and "Man Precepter" was written down in the *catterlog* of books belonging to the Sandy Creek Literary Society.

[Another pause.]

Prest.—Come, now, Mr. Secretary, it is your time. Please to name some book.

The Secretary, thus exhorted, named *"Pope's Asses,"** and being adopted by a formal vote, was duly registered in the "catterlog."

Just about this time, a disturbance among the horses that had been hitched to the surrounding bushes, which had from time to time saluted their ears, became so uproarious, that more than one of the members began to look through the cracks of the log house to see what was going on. At this instant, BILL JENKINS, a white headed, widemouthed boy, a good deal noted for his propensity for *devilment* and fun, rushed into the house, and said, in a squealing voice—

"The Pre-Pre-President's sta-sta-stallion has broke loose among the hosses down yander, and is ra-rarin' and pi-pi-pitchin', and a kickin', like all wrath!"

This announcement, confirmed as it was by a still louder squeal from without, had the effect temporarily to dissolve this literary conclave in a very abrupt manner; for the President, forgetting for once his dignity, rushed out of the meeting house, followed by the Society (men, women, and boys), and proceeded to the scene of confusion. Here, sure enough, the Squire's steed was loose among the other horses. This animal, which had no claim to the immunity which it enjoyed, except that he was pied or particolored, like a circus horse, was nevertheless a great pet of his master's, and like most other pets, was spiteful and vicious. He was now giving full vent to this unamiable quality, running first to one horse and then to another, biting, pawing, kicking most furiously.

"Help me, gents," said Ben, "help me catch Selim, or he will kill some of your harses! He is a powerful crittur! Come, Mr. Thompson, help me catch him! Look! he is going right to you harse, and he will pretty nigh devour that small animal of yours!"

"Let him try it!" said Thompson, quietly; "Grubber can kick a fence rail in two every pop, and has such a slight with his hind feet that he can put the print of his shoes in the same spot upon the fore gate of a wagon, three times hand runnin', without varyin' half an inch!"

Now this same Grubber was a black, roughlooking pony, that seemed to know that danger was approaching him in the rear; for he backed his ears, and drew his hinder legs a little more under him. Selim made right at him "like all wrath," as Bill Jenkins had stated, his mouth wide open, his nostrils distended, and a terrible fury glowing in his eye; it did seem as if he was about to finish the diminutive Grubber at a single gulp.

"Help! gentlemen!" said Ben, as he saw his fiery steed getting nearer his antagonist—"Selim will kill that little harse!"

"Never fear for Grubber," said Thompson—"he'll take care of himself."

Just at this moment, Grubber let fly with his hind feet, and a sharp clear crack gave assurance that Selim had *got it* on his cranium. He recoiled for a moment, and seemed either stunned, or, may be, had stopped to *consider*! But on the next moment, with redoubled fury he returned to the charge. This time he had the sense not to come up right behind Grubber, but took him, as the sailors say, upon "the lee quarter." This seemed to suit Grubber as well as the other mode of battle, for suddenly whirling his hind parts into the line of approach, he gave his assailant such a *clew* upon the under jaw, that Selim was fain to retire from the conflict.

"Obstupu-et steterunt que comoe et vox faucibus haesit."*

"Indeed," said Thompson, "Ben had to feed his horse on meal and water for two weeks afterwards."

But again to the Society. This interruption being over, the Society again assembled—the President, something disconcerted himself, made an apology for his discomfited favorite. He had "never known Selim in such a *ridiculous* scrape before: he never had been known to slip the bridle before and he was much inclined to sespect that that uneducated varmunt Bill Jenkins, had turned him loose on purpose to see him get hurt by that devilish brute of Thampson's. You all seed," he continued, "how that chap chuckled and grinned when that unaccountable brute of Thampson's had well nigh broke my harse's jaw. But let us get on with our business. Mr. Thampson, you seem to be in a mighty good humor, will you be so good as name some book?"

The individual thus accosted for a moment looked grave—but as he was a subscriber, and had thus far participated in the proceedings and enjoyed them, he thought it would never do to back out. But what book was he to name? He had seen many books in his lifetime (that is, the backs of them,) and Dr. B., who resided at his house, had a great many, but for the life of him he could remember the title of only one; and that was "Wistar's Ana-tomy," so that he was, perforce, as it were, obliged to propose that.

Prest.—Anny and Tommy; well, I appose the sanctioning of that namination. Not that I know what the nature of the aforesaid book is, but judging from the name of it, and from the nature and character of the proposer, I suppose it is some of that light trash called navels—I therefore hope it will be rejected.

This was enough; the vote was taken, and Mr. Thompson's proposal rejected *unanimously*.

By this time, however, the business seemed to get on better—various books were thought of by the remaining members, and as none of these happened to own unconquerable Grubbers, their "naminations" all passed muster—and the *catterlog* of the Sandy Creek Literary Society, which was long after preserved by our informant, as a literary curiosity, as well as a voucher for his own correctness, exhibits in the category of "ancient and madern history"—

Hyssop's Fabbles*	Pol and Verginy,*
Wats Sams and hims,*	Pixe Rethmetic,*
Duncans Kikkors,*	Joolus Seeser,
Roberson Cruso,	Life of Murl (Murrell),
Plessurs of Hop,*	Skotch Lessens (Scott's lessons)
Moner Kumferted,*	&c. &c. &c.

The main business of the day being thus happily over, it was now nearly night, but Benjamin was a leader in the Sandy Creek Church, and being a practised exhorter, and a strong holder forth in prayer, proposed that an undertaking so praiseworthy and commendable as that they were engaged in then, should be finished "by raising their hearts to the Lord." They accordingly all kneeled down, and Ben at once dashed off into a long rattling prayer, which we will not undertake to repeat, or further to describe, but must hasten to the finale of this story. Before we get through, however, it is necessary for us to tell that Bill Jenkins had, on the day before, been rambling in the woods, and coming across a small hornet's nest, he slyly approached it, and having knocked off the sentinel hornet from the mouth or entrance, with a small stick, he incontinently made prisoners of all the fraternity within; stopping the entrance of the nest with a paper wad, he safely took it off from its position, and all that day had carried it in his coat pocket.

It so happened that when the motion was made for prayer, Bill's place was right behind the President, and not very far from him. While this holy exercise was going on, the eye of this urchin, in wandering about, happened to descry a small pocket that had been formed by the ripping of a few pleats of the President's pantaloons, from that functionary's waistband. It must be premised, also, that the weather was warm, and therefore the President was in his shirt sleeves, and *therefore* it was that this prying Jackanapes was enabled to discern this imperfection in the 'Squire's wardrobe.

There it was, standing most invitingly open. What a nice opportunity to get rid of his hornet's nest! thought Bill. It was getting dark, too.

"I don't like the spoutin little rascal no how. If Jack Riddle, my master, wouldn't always make me go to his night meetings, and listen to his long prayers, I wouldn't care."

The fact was, Bill's knees had already begun to ache—he had been down on the bare floor for a solid half hour, and this determined him. He looked again at the open chasm—he got ready with his hornet's nest, and resolved to *go it*, and abide the consequences. Just as he had come to this conclusion the prayer was finished, and in the confusion of rising, Bill pitched the nest into this most tempting receptacle, and at the same instant dexterously unstopped it.

Prayer being over, our Squire proposed a few words of practical improvement before they parted.

"I don't know how you feel, my brethren," said Ben, "but I feel [here he cringed] as if—the Lord [slap] had done something for my soul!"

By this time there was warm work in the back settlements. But vanity and zeal, when roused to a high pitch, are proof (for a while, at least,) against many of the ills we suffer in the flesh. Ben, at every word, however, screwed and twisted, and slapped the affected part of his person.

"I feel [slap]—I feel [wriggle]—the—a—Spirit—of grace in—

a—my bosom—and"—[here a deadly paleness came over his face—
it was too much—Ben forgot himself in his agony, and wound up
the sentence with]—"and—and—*h-ll fire in my breeches!*" delivered
in a loud tone of voice, accompanied with an energetic slap upon
his lower back with both hands.

The meeting adjourned *sine die*,* and as Baron Duberly* would
say, "promiscuously."

The joke went abroad, and every one present got sore with
laughing, saving and excepting the aforesaid Benjamin Primm,
Esquire, the President. He, encased in his sevenfold shield of vanity,
was proof against ridicule. He advertised another meeting at the
same place, but no one came but Bill Jenkins and another. In fact,
that learned fraternity, the "Sandy Creek Literary Society," never
met again, and all that remains to tell of its *fuit** is the aforesaid
"catterlog," which fell into our friend Thompson's hands, and
henceforth shall have a place in the curiosities of literature.

The Spirit of the Times, August 15, 1846, pp. 289–290.

THE ROUND ROBIN

By the author of "Cousin Sally Dilliard," Etc. Etc.

Some years ago all the Lawyers attending ——Court (North Carolina,) boarded at the house of Mr. B——, who, at the beginning of his career as a publican, was assiduous and provident: but riches multiplied, and our boniface became lazy, crusty, and parsimonious. His accommodation (as it is generally called,) from being the very best in the circuit, degenerated by degrees into the very worst. This was borne for years, with mutterings of dissatisfaction from time to time, 'tis true, but still borne with until their patience became exhausted. They had a formal meeting, and after gravely talking the matter over, resolved to leave him, and go in a body to another tavern, in the same village. The duty of announcing their determination was devolved upon one of the "brethren," who, stuck with the ridiculous aspect and mock importance the affair had assumed, wrote the following, and, signing all their names to it in a round ring, sent it to their landlord:—

A DECLARATION.

When in the course of human events it became necessary for a hungry, half-fed, imposed on set of men, to dissolve the bonds of Landlord and Boarder, a decent respect for the opinions of mankind, requires that they should declare the causes which have impelled them to this separation.

We hold these truths to be self-evident: that all men are created with mouths and stomachs, and that they are endowed by their Creator with certain inalianable rights, among which is that no man shall be compelled to starve out of mere complaisance to a landlord; and that every man has a right to fill his stomach and wet his whistle with the best that's going. The history of the present landlord of the White Lion, is a history of repeated insults, exactions, and injuries, all having, in direct object the establishment of absolute tyranny over their stomachs and throats. To prove this, let facts be submitted to a candid world:—

He has refused to keep any thing to drink but ball-faced whiskey.

He has refused to set upon his table for dinner any thing but turnip soup, with a little bull-beef* and sourkrout, which are not wholesome and necessary for the public good.

He has refused to let his only waiter, *Blink-eyed Joe*, put more than six grains of coffee to one gallon of water.

He has turned loose a multitude of fleas and swarms of bed-bugs, to assail us in the peaceable hours of the night, and to eat out our substance.

He has kept up in our beds and bedsteads standing armies of these merciless savages, with their scalping knives and tomahawks, whose known rule of warfare is undistinguished destruction.

He has excited domestic insurrections among us, by getting drunk before breakfast, and making his wife and servants so before dinner, whereby there has often been the devil to pay.

He has waged cruel war against nature itself, by feeding our horses with broom straw and corn stalks, and carrying them off to drink at puddles, where swine refused to wallow.

He has protected One-eyed Joe in his villany, in the robbery of our jugs, by pretending to give him a mock trial, after sharing with him the spoil.

He has cut off our trade with foreign parts, and brought in his own stinking whiskey when we had sent him to buy better liquor abroad, and with a perfidy scarce paralleled in the most barbarous ages, he has been known to drink up our foreign spirits and fill up our bottles with his own dire potions.

He has imposed taxes upon us to an enormous amount, against our consent, and without any rule but his own arbitrary will and pleasure.

A Landlord whose character is thus marked by every act which may define a tyrant and a pinch-gut,* is unfit to keep a boarding house for Cherokee Indians.

Nor have we been wanting in our attentions to Mrs. B.—and Miss SALLY. We have warned them from time to time of the attempts of B—— to starve and to fleece us. We have reminded them of the circumstances of our coming to board with them. We have appealed to their nature, justice, and magnanimity. We have conjured them to alter a state of things which would inevitably interrupt our connexion and correspondence. They, too, have been deaf to the voice of justice. We are, therefore, constrained to hold all three of these parties, alike inimical to our well being and regardless of our comforts.

We, therefore, make this solemn declaration of our final separation from our former Landlord, and cast our defiance into his teeth.

The Spirit of the Times, August 22, 1846, p. 301.

THE FRENCHMAN AND HIS MENAGERIE

Written for the 'Spirit,' by the author of

'Cousin Sally Dilliard.'

The town of Jefferson, in Ashe County, N.C., is a neat little village, situated on a small plain, between three lofty mountains-the Negro, the Phoenix, and the Paddy. The country is newly settled, in comparison with other portions of the State; and not many years ago, the inhabitants were not of the 'law and order' party, by any means. The following history of a Frenchman and his menagerie, will pretty clearly elucidate that assertion. It may be relied on as correct, for the facts were all proven in the Superior Court of that county, on the trial of an indictment for a riot, against about twenty of the persons engaged in the 'fun.' Well, now, to our narrative.

This Frenchman had had a respectable caravan of living animals, but the winter proving very severe, their Asiatic natures gave way, and many of them died. The enterprising stranger patched up his assortment as well as he could; however, he got a bear from the mountains of Virginia in the vicinage,* a panther, and a wild cat, and divers domestic creatures, not very common in these wild parts; such as an ass, and a goat, of an uncommon color, and an extraordinary beard. In copartnership with our Fenchman was a talking Yankee, who made up in vocabulary and slang for what he

lacked in *show*. Upon the whole they had got on passably well, but
here at Jefferson affairs with them took a sad reverse. In the first
place, it was objected by the crowd that the price of admission was
too high for a new country.

"I would have to give only a quarter," said big Bill Reaves, "to
see the Elephant, and here you have advertised a South American
Tiger, and a Tropical Bar, and a few ring tail Monkies, and you
pretend to ask that price. But you must come down to 12½ cents,
else you will get no customers here."

And the outsiders seconded the motion. But the proprieter of the
"Grand, Beautiful, and Rare Exhibition," insisted upon "de twenty-
five cent."

"You nevair did see sooch ting in all your life time—coom in
gentlehem and see de grand display."

"You hear that?" said Bill; "why, that is clever for a Frenchman!
he says we may all come in for nothing. Walk in, boys—come on,
all of you! Didn't you hear him ask us in?"

And thereupon he raised a shout, as did several of his backers,
keeping up such a din and hurrahing as to drown the remonstrances
of the European, who was endeavoring to explain that they were all
welcome for "de money." Five or six strong, stout, dare-devil
mountaineers, who would have wrenched old Neptune's trident
from his hands, and kicked Jupiter down Olympus, if anything like
cruelty had been required of them, rushed by the agitated Frenchman, the last one of whom he was so incautious as to thrust gently
back with his hand; this worthy wopped him, and sent him reeling
from his position. Before poor Crapeau* had regained his feet and
brushed the dirt from his clothes, (for that is an office the Frenchman never forgets,) the whole crowd of rowdies and bullies had
entered. He remained outside deploring his wrongs and his loss of
profits. I heard him say, "Dis de land of liberty. I ting so ver much.
He take great liberty wid de stranger."

After venting his feeling in vain ejaculations, the Frenchman
thought he had as well go inside of his canvass tabernacle and see
how things were going on there.

"Is that what you call the South American Tiger?" said one.

"Yes sair," said the Frenchman, "and he be ver fine Tigree. Take care, gentle'm, you no go too close, he devour you entire."

"He devour!" said another. "Why, d—n it, he is nothing but a Black Mountain *Paynter*, and if you will turn him out we'll whip him."

The proposition, though lightly made, was earnestly seconded by some half dozen. The Frenchman begged and protested, and threatened that they would all very soon be destroyed if they were so imprudent as to turn loose so dangerous an animal. But notwithstanding all this, and notwithstanding some screeching and squalling among the women and children, the declaration was succeeded by the act, and in an instant 'The Grand South American Tiger' was in the middle of them. It seems that for a moment he was not decided what use he should make of his liberty, so unexpectedly obtained. He made a glance around him, of rather doubtful significance, and would doubtless have proceeded further to consider, when his liberators promptly decided the question for him. Bill Reaves first planted a sledge-hammer blow right between his eyes. Hiram Ray gave him a horse kick on one side; while Douglas Dickson gave him another on the other side. Then kicks and licks, and cuffs and stamps, came down upon him so thick and heavy, that the poor brute, making one effort to disengage himself, jumped back into his cage, and fairly groaned in the spirit. A shout of victory went up from the human side of the question.

The proprietor, Mons. Ponte Feezle, made every sort of grimace and expostulation, but was told if he interfered with *their show* they would feed him away to the wild beasts.

They next proceeded to bring the big monkey and the catamount* in contact. After a hard fight, amid much clamor, and many offers to bet on either side, the catamount fastened upon the throat of his adversary, and held on until the vital spark in the poor monkey was extinguished.

They then swore they would try the catamount for murder. They thereupon adjourned to the Court House, carrying with them the accused, whom, or rather which, they placed in the prisoner's box, and formally accused him of murder. A Judge took his seat on the bench, a jury was empanelled, and counsel appeared for the prisoner and for the State. The jury went out to deliberate, the court to liquor, and the Sheriff fell asleep beside the prisoner, being *whole seas over*. The jury could not agree whether their verdict should be monkey slaughter or murder. To settle the difference, it was proposed that the two smallest men on either side should decide it by a fight. This wager of battle fell to the lot of one of the Rararks and one of the Sextons. We forget which way the fight went, or what was the verdict; indeed, we believe it never was given in, for when the court reassembled, it was found that some intermeddler had slipped into the court house, and had hanged the catamount until he was dead, dead, dead!!

The Spirit of the Times, March 16, 1850, p.44.

ABEL HUCKS IN A TIGHT PLACE

By the Author of "Cousin Sally Dilliard."

Monroe, Union Co., N.[C.], July 4th, 1851

---

*Mister Porter**—I wishes to lay a case before you that I thinks is hard. You see I was born a poor man, and luck has been agin me ever sense I was born; and what's worse, the law has been agin me, too. I mout* have stole several times, and not been found out, but that's agin my prinsipples. I don't see how them as gets rich by stealing can enjoy their riches—I couldn't do it, and so I wouldn't steal. I mout have lugged* and loafed about as some does, but I'm above that, too; so I has suffered some in this world, and I allows to suffer some more before I'll either steal or lug. But that's not to the pint—or rather to the *half-pint:* for the worst pint in my case was a *half-pint* to begin with. I 'spose I had drunk about that quantity of the ardent,* when who should come along but *"Forty-foot Houston."* Now, Mr. P., it so happens that I am a *low man* in inches, and I can't bear for one of those tall fellows to be looking over my head at something beyond me. Ses I:

"Mr. Houston, look some other course."

Ses he: "What's the matter, Hucks?"

Ses I: "I don't wan't you to be a standin' thar a lookin' over my hed."

"Why," ses he, "Hucks, you are a fool!"

That was enuff; I had allers wanted to *hit* a tall man, and "Forty-foot" was the highest I had ever seen. So I goes up and jags him in the short ribs. Ses he:

"Quit, Hucks!—you are a fool!"

Well, upon that I digs into him agin. Well, then at last Mister Houston gets mad, and takes me by the two arms, and gives me a shake that made my teeth chatter and my eyes strike fire, and he hands me over the fence to a constable, and *he* takes me down to Sabett's cross roads, where the Court was held in a masheen [machine] house, and Lawyer "Joolus" was employed to defend me. He is a mighty goodharted man, Joolus is, and so is Judge Battle* that tried me; but there was no chance for me to get off, and so I 'fesses guilty, and Joolus turns *into* beggin' the Judge. He said I was a poor unfortunate man, with six children, and a little given to liker; and there was no jail nigher than Charlotte, and it would never do to send me to jail.

"Has you got any stocks here?" ses the Judge to the Sheriff.

"No, sur," ses the Sheriff; "this is the second Court ever held in the County of Union, and we ain't reddy with sich things yet."

Well, I felt a bit of relief when I heard the Sheriff's anser, and the Judge looked down at a piece of paper, and then he says—

"Mr. Clerk, record the judgment of the Court: Let Mr. Hucks be confined in the stocks for one hour. And," says he, "Mr. Sheriff, you can come as near as possible to executing the judgment of the Court."

"How is that?" says Joolus, flaring up and looking wrathly at the Judge. "Your honor don't mean to inflict any unusual punishment?"

"Oh, no!" says the Judge, laffin; "the mode of carrying out the sentence is left to the Sheriff."

And then all the lawyers laft, but Joolus—and some said *"fence, Joolus,"* and so [Joolus] got madder still, and says: "Mr. Sheriff, I dare you to do that!"

And so they took me out of the Courthouse on a general laff, and as the lawyers came along to dinner, thar I was lying with both legs through the crack of a rail fence, and some fellers setting on the fence making sport of me!

And I heard that queer-looking feller, "Ham Jones," say—
"Joolus, *look* at your client!"

And then I thought Joolus would have fainted. He turned to the
Judge, and he says: "My God, Judge! I never had a client in sich a
fix before!"

And the Judge and all of them lawyers laughed out. But I felt
hurt—my feelings was hurt as well as my legs. I don't know
whether or not you are a lawyer, but I want to know whether it is
accordin' to the American Constitution, to put a fellers legs through
a rail fence because they haven't got stocks in a new county? I want
to know, sir! for ef that be according to the constitution, I'll go
across the line to South Carolina and help to make a new constitution!"

Yors to command,

ABEL HUCKS.

The Spirit of the Times, August 23, 1851, p. 316.

Omnibus Contributions and Miscellaneous

INTRODUCTION

Ham Jones is seen at his most antic in many of his short *Carolina Watchman* contributions published under the heading of "Salisbury Omnibus." Rural Southern weekly papers in the 1830s typically gave almost no local news. What local news was included, with national and international news and with political editorials, was certainly seldom presented with comic flair. Jones's Omnibus pieces, then, were unusual, for his observations range from comic accounts of life in Salisbury to literary spoofing in his poem about the killing of the hog. Some of his jokes are political, others are racial—in one, which uses black dialect, the intent is to show that abolitionists did not understand the peculiar institution of slavery. He was openly contemptuous of a political preacher, and he obviously enjoyed exposing the humbuggery of a phrenologist. These Omnibus pieces began on July 8, 1837, and continued until a short time before he sold the paper.

This section also contains two miscellaneous items—a short law story called "Dog Suit" and the dialect poem "Perley Poore." "Dog Suit" at first seems to be a description of a case involving the poisoning of a dog, and it contains some humorous comments about the testimony of a witness. The writer then turns to the undercurrent of the story—lovers who have been kept apart by a watchful dog and a grandmother, and whose course of love remains thwarted, even after the dog is poisoned. The writer does not seem to know why the girl married someone else, and the anecdote, with its strange twist, is merely tantalizing. The dialogue sounds as if it were written by Jones, but the story is not signed.

"Perley Poore" is a dialect poem about the lost Whig political cause. Millard Fillmore, the Whig who served as president after Zachary Taylor's death, attempted to take the Whig party to the middle ground on the issue of slavery, but the divisions in the country were already too great for him to succeed. He failed, just as he failed to get the Whig nomination for the presidency in 1852. His career as a Whig was over—the Whig party was itself dying—but he became active in the Know-Nothing party and was nominated by that party for the presidency in 1856. In that effort he was supported by many of the remaining Whigs, but his cause—and the Whig cause—were lost. That lost cause and Perley's penance are the background for the poem. Jones several times reprinted dialect poems of James Russell Lowell and is probably indebted to Lowell in this work.

SALISBURY OMNIBUS

1.

The heat during this week has been quite intense, often as high as
92 degrees (Far.) and the weather quite favorable for harvesting.
Corn grows with great rapidity. Flour sells here at $6. Corn at 75
cents, cotton at about 7 (little done). The town is quite healthy and
the country around scarcely less so. Our town girls look beautiful,
notwithstanding the pressure on their ribs! they however take a
good deal of exercise as well on horse back as on foot: pony riding,
and dancing being quite the rage during the solstice. Our beaux
(foreign and domestic) are sprightly looking chaps, but they don't
seem to get a head: at least one would conclude so from the
barrenness of hymenial intelligence. Travelling through here is
rather at a low ebb. Since money has become scarcer or rather worse
in South Carolina, the state has either become much more healthy,
or their own springs improved greatly in *medicinal virtues* . . . Our
Female School is flourishing. Our Court Dockets are small. Our jail
is empty, and so is *our* pocket. Thus our readers have a sketch of
what's going on here and hereabouts (July 8, 1837, p. 3).

2.

Ridin on a Rail.—In our last, we spoke of a fashion, prevalent with
the ladies, of Pony-riding: since then, the fashion has somewhat

83

changed and rail-riding with the Gentleman has taken its place.—
To explain: On last Monday night a bustle in the street attracted
our notice about 10 o'clock, and on going forth to see what was the
matter we saw a *fellow* mounted on a rail without a saddle or
martingale, leisurely parading down the street accompanied by a
body guard, who marched to the tune of "Raccoon on the rail,"*
&c. It seems that this "bold dragoon" was taken up at a place where
his marriage vow was not likely to be signally honored, and
forwarded *per express* a part of the way home. We dare say but for the
name of riding, he had just as soon walked.

Query—Would not a state of sus-pense been better?

N. B. On the next night the little boys of this place improved
upon the above fashion, by parading a *man of straw* through the
town upon a rail to the same tune.—An old fashioned old field
school has been got up in this town since our last, we hope upon
Solomon's maxim "spare the rod, &c." Any one who will go to
Church and observe how *barbarously* the heads of certain of our
fashionables have been manipulated, will acknowledge an *aching*
necessity for a Barber in Salisbury. . . .

The following dialogue between two *sable Gents,* which was
overheard the other evening in our streets, deserves a place in the
Omnibus for its *truth.* We commend it to the consideration of the
Abolition Societies at the North.

Peter—What you dung do wid dat dare money dat old Misses
give you tudder day.

Tom—Why I lay him out in candy and beer.

Peter—Why Tom how you afford to buy sich nic nacs durin the
pressure.*

Tom—Why bless you Peter, can't a gentman 'dulge in de *nic nacs*
what has got a master bound to him for the *necessaries* of life (July
15, 1837, p. 3)?

3.

Phrenology, Humbuggery, &c.—A Yankee by the name of Alcott,*
who has been a Preacher, after studying Phrenology for three weeks
as he himself declared in a public talk, has betaken himself to the

money-making trade of putting vain people in a good humor with themselves by praising their skull bones, and by attributing to them powers and qualities which no one else ever dreamed of. For each examination he charges one dollar, and as vanity and credulity are the weaknesses of poor human nature at which his arts are levelled, it may be well believed that he drives a profitable business. We do not pretend to say, that there is nothing in Phrenology. We have not sufficiently attended to the subject to form an opinion one way or the other, and as we think a man's character and abilities can better be determined by his conduct and conversation, we have no notion of bestowing even the necessary three weeks to the study. But we do say that Dr. Alcott is a *humbug*. Any one capable of uttering in the form of a lecture so much fustian and absurdity as he did here on last Monday night is *an arrant humbug*.

By the English constitution whoever marries Queen Victoria will have to be her subject.—Hereabouts this is a good deal the fate of husbands without the sanction of such high authority. Since the hoisting of one clever girl over the heads of so many sensible men, we are apprehensive that the whole female race—young and old— ugly and pretty, will take a second growth: Attention then, the whole!—Married men, Bachelors and Beaus. Hold up your heads. Look the threatened tyranny in the face, and if they do advance upon you, squeeze their little soul cases out of them.

Shooting matches for mutton are getting to be the fashionable amusement amongst certain of our citizens. If hard dollars were put up for targets, we know a chap or two that could hold a steady sight on them.

Some wags have proposed that the spruce old Beau, Van Buren,* should try his magical powers of negotiation in patching up a treaty of alliance with the Belle Queen of England. Perhaps it was with some such sneaking notion that he talked so largely about the "Kinderhook family"* when among the nobility of England. We dare say that KING MARTY* would grace the presence chamber of Queen Vicky quite as handsomely as the German importations, on which the Royal family of England have generally depended for matrimonial splices. It would be no doubt quite as much to his taste as the splendor of the East Room, and, if he could take Dick

Johnson* and his sables with him, we, for one, would rejoice at the riddance. . . .

The mint at Charlotte will soon be completed. The officers and operatives have all assembled, we learn, with the exception of the Assayer.—The salaries are all going on but *no mint drops* going out. As the mines have nearly blown out, and not even enough gold can be borrowed by the Government to make a show with, it is thought that this Institution will be converted into a branch of Mr. Woodbury's* Treasury Bank to issue protected drafts for the better currency (August 5, 1837, p. 3).

4.

Who is the gentleman sportsman, that went hunting not a month ago, and got "so unco happy" as to *take a drink of gunpowder* under the supposition that he was enjoying the contents of his liquor flask? The gentleman is known to us, but we must throw the responsibility of divulging his name on himself . . .

Green Corn Suppers. We have heard of the Indian ceremony of the green corn dance. But some of our town "Bucks" have improved on the idea: they have green corn suppers. The *style* and *finish* of the thing we have not exactly understood, but the idea of going to bed with a stomach crammed with green corn is enough to give one an apoplexy.

We know of a jury charged to try an affray between two men that was hung a long time. They were divided on the question thus: *six* were for acquitting, *five* for finding the defendant not guilty, and *one for making the parties fight it over again. The King's English.*—A fellow once wishing to settle the estate of a deceased brother, and to be appointed guardian to his infant children, went to the office of a lawyer and told him he wished to "insult" him and was able to pay for it. After some explanation he proceeded: "My brother died detested, and left two little infidels, I want to know if I can be appointed their executioner."

SEQUEL

Monsieur Jean,

SAIRE: You tink you dam smart to have every body stuck up in the Omniboos—Dare you [the page is mutilated] I tell you vat, I tink it verry "rascaille," and den if the Omniboos man open his mouth, the gentlehome take his pistol and he shoot him down, so saire you better mind. You call dis de land of libertee—de land of Grand Repooblicans: vell I tink very pretty land, where the town constab let de hog, and de dog, and de sheep, and de cow jis walk about as big as he please, and let de Editor jis say what he pleases about any body in de Omniboos. You call Jackson von great man, but what is he in compare wid de grand Monarque Henri, and your leetel sheep shank of a diminish Presiden Van Buren [page mutilated] Look at dis dam town. Why you know put him in de Omnibus? You put de flea, and de fly, and de bug in de market-hoose, and you hab de cow wid de bell on in de street going ting, ting, ting all night, and you hab de cat goin yaw, yaw, yaw, and de Jack Ass make such noise I neber did see, and you hab de gon and de pistol goin bang so dere is no such ting as Miss Nongtong get her natural res. Den dere is dat dam letel oogly indecent hos vat your own oogly neeger ride about, and call him von race hos, den dere is one sight of oogly women in dis town, what make you put in de pretty one, and leave de oogly one out. Now saire you mus put in dis letter else I cus de whole consarne of de Omniboos. PIERE DE NONGTONG (August 26, 1837, p. 3).

5.

We received a long poetic contribution from an anonymous source at Statesville, with a request that we should publish it as long as we could afford to do so for the money sent, but as *there was none of that* if it had not been for the poetic merit of the article itself, we should have permitted it to "waste its fragrance on the desert air."

The following excerpt, it must be confessed, shows a talent for the descriptive:

> "Another sin I had forgot:
> I aimed the brickbat at his head
> When I went up I found it dead,
> I quickly drew him to the gate:
> And there a while on him did wait:

> I tried to get him to stand up,
> But found with him the jigg was up:
> I told the neighbors all along
> That he got foundered there on corn
> But now they have it sung about,
> I killed him there and threw him out."

Now it must be admitted that 'long' and 'corn' do not ryme as well as 'up' and 'up.' But what is the *poetic licentia* for but to help out in such matters? Upon the whole, it is an admirable production. The idea of the fellow's trying to get the hog to stand up after he had knocked it 'speechless' with a brickbat is truly graphic. Try it again, Fipenny!* and take this wonderful poem of Nick Bottom's* for thy pattern.

> Then Phebal's car,
> Shall shine from far,
> And make and mar
> The stubborn fates.

Another.—A Gentleman about five feet 2 with a duncolored fustian frock coat on, a little tar'd and greasy, stepped up to a writing desk at Col. Long's tavern, and with a very businesslike manner asked for some paper: and being furnished withal, he proceeded in a kind of enraptured air to figure forth a heart which he duly slashed vertically and horizontally with black lines: underneath which he wrote the following soul touching strains,

> "Sigh poor heart,
> But do not break,
> Deep in love but
> Dare to speak
> Better to sigh and
> Suffer pain than
> Love and be not loved again."

Having thus poured forth these thrilling sentiments, from a surcharged bosom, he made his bow and mounting his saddle horse he gracefully took his long single line in his left hand, while with the other he threw off an explosion from his whip lash equal to the report of a horseman's pistol, and slowly took his departure to the tune of 'ge-ep wae jolly.'* The whole scene was gone through with the utmost gravity, and non chalence. Is he not a case?—Go it tobacco-worm!

A thrifling fellow came into a store in this town not long since, and behaving quite rudely, was ordered to leave it: instead of doing so, he let off with a volly of foul language on the store keeper. Whereupon the merchant cooly walked from behind the counter, and gave the fellow a kick which sent him a step or two towards the door: this he followed up with another, which impelled him a little further in his onward course: he then made a slight pause when his copartner called out 'once more dear friend unto the breach,' whereupon the intruder was hurried with a third application of the kind, face foremost to the street pavement (November 4, 1837, p. 3).

6.

Not bad.—In a County Court last week, was tried a suit of trespass brought against three patrollers for whipping a slave without authority: The plantiff's counsel in the course of a pretty heavy denunciation against patrollers, observed that "dressed with a little brief authority, like an angry ape, they cut such fantastic capers before high Heaven, as made angels weep." A waggist Attorney sitting by, whispered to one of his brethern, "I think the angels would have been more apt to laugh at such a likeness" (December 2, 1837, p. 3).

7.

Queen of May.—This annual fete was celebrated by the young ladies of Mrs. Hutchison's School, on last Tuesday, quite handsomely. Miss Rachel Troy, of Columbus Co. was the fair representative of the vernal goddess, attended by a suitable number of flower-bedecked maids of Honor, one of whom, Miss Isabella Troy, of Randolph, delivered to her Majesty on the throne, a very pretty and appropriate address, and another, Miss Elizabeth Allen, of Charleston, bestowed the blooming coronet. The whole affair was quite beautiful, & passed off well.

Counterpart. The male urchins of the village, than whom there is not a sharper set of chaps, at all sorts of fun and mischief, understanding in the morning that the coronation was not to take place, determined that the day should not pass uncelebrated. So they took up a barefooted companion of theirs, and crowned him with a magnificent wreath of *snowballs.* Him they carried through the streets under an arch of flowers, *riding on a rail*, escorted by a train of barefooted boys cutting all kinds of antics to the tune of 'Racoon on the rail,'* accompanied with the music of a tin pan. . . .

Police.—We have received several complaints for the Omnibus, against the Police of this village, among which is the increased and increasing number of swine infesting our streets, and among others, we are overhauled for our particular share of dereliction in this particular. For ourself, we *"fess judgment,"* and promise a reform. We have been *flea bitten* into a sense of duty in this matter, and have already commenced the work of *killing off the long-faced gentry**, pertaining to our premises. We call upon our neighbors to do likewise, for the evil is really getting to be intolerable. We must ask of the commissioners to save the ancient borough of Salisbury from the threatened soubriquet of *Hogtown.* If no other mode can be adopted, let a commission issue to Jim Archy, to *seek and slay*, and we will warrant a disappearance of the evil.

We are also requested to call the attention of our police officers, to the practice prevalent in some parts of the town, of suffering cattle to remain in the streets at night.

We learn from good authority, that the old lady who abused the race-horses to us in such energetic terms the other day, *went to sleep in church the very Sunday afterwards, and slept a good half hour, under one of the best sermons that has been delivered in this town, for a twelve-month.* We understand also, that her daughter was there, clad in black silk stockings with a *hole in one of them* just above the shoe mouth, *as big as a ten cent piece.* We think she had better darn the hole in her own morals, and the hole in her daughter's black stockings, before she becomes so critical about the rents in other people's conduct.

BIRTHS—A corrrespondent suggests the propriety of adopting in our local papers, the European custom of publishing *births* as well as Marriages and Deaths. For our part, we are willing to go to any extent in this respect that may be agreeable to the ladies. We will even anticipate for them by stating expectancies, if they wish it be done: But in those family matters, we can not dare to venture on new modes without the consent of these fair arbiters. *Dux femina facti.* The meaning of which is, that the "grey mare is the better horse," in the article of fashion. . . .

Our contemporary of the Standard is informed, that we have no need for nostrums of any kind, and therefore, we did not *take* the dose which he prepared and sent abroad with such a high commendation of its virtues. Our objection was to the Physician more than to the medicine, for the mixture appeared so much like a preparation of *chalk and water*, that we were not much afraid of it: but we could not consent to let a disciple of Doctor Jackson* try experiments upon our poor carcass. The old man himself has well nigh cured the nation to death with his *wonderful sanatives*, and therefore, we must distrust all who have taken out Patents under him . . . (May 5, 1838, p. 3).

8.

Remedial. A friend of ours suggests that hereafter if young ladies should discover holes in their black silk stockings just as they are dressing for Church, and their mothers should be too conscientious to darn them, they had better adopt the Chapel Hill remedy, i.e., black the skin with ink opposite to the hole. This is one of the *grandest discoveries of modern times* (May 12, 1838, p. 3).

9.

A Medical gentleman of the Whig party, was not long since addressing a meeting of the people, when an impertinent Loco of the lower class, who had been *put up to it by his betters*, called out to him in the most animated part of his discourse, "Halloo Doctor, what will you ax to pull my tooth." "When I get through" said the other, "I will pull your tooth for a shilling, and your nose for nothing." He didn't venture against that snag any more in *the sequel* as old Mark says.

The chap that sent us the account of the death of *Mrs. Simeon D. Pemberton*, thought that he was extra smart. He ought to be ashamed of sporting with such *grave* matters, if he was not ashamed of imposing upon the credulity of an editor. Mr. P. never was married, and therefore had no wife to die. This was a very poor hoax, and a very dirty attack on private character. But Mr. Pemberton has the original letter sent us, and we hope will make the author of it smoke for it. . . .

At one of the best taverns in the State of North Carolina, the outer gate is fastened with a piece of trace chain put over a nail in the inside. You have to get half over the gate before you can reach it. We had given fair notice to the owner of this property to fix his fastenings better, else we would ride him in the Omnibus. Next time we will *cart* him. . . .

Shortly previous to the last presidential election, the Editor of this paper went to the Hatter's shop (7 miles off) & made a speech in favor of the Whig candidate, Judge White. As soon as he was done, an old friend of his took him one side, & the following dialogue took place. "Jones" says our friend, "we dont know anything about these men you have been talkin about, and we dont know how about votin for em.—'Spose you come out yourself. Every man of us will go for you down this way." "Why Jake! I am too poor a man to bear the expense of electioneering on such a grand scale. My pocket would give out before I had treated one fourth of the nation." "Ah that indeed" said our friend, and he seemed puzzled: he kept repeating "that indeed" "that indeed" at length starting from his reverie, he says *"well Jones: since you cant offer for President spose you come out for sheriff* (September 29, 1838, p. 3).

10.

William A. Morris, A *Republican* Baptist Preacher, is the Loco foco* candidate for Congress in the Cumberland district, and from the lucubrations of a writer in the N. Carolinian, we preceive that the party are making calculations on the "divine" influence of their candidate's vocation. Well! there is an advantage in *stumping* it to God and *praying* to the people. The political preacher occupies the confines of two worlds—he lives about where Earth meets Heaven, (if there be any such place,) and like the hot pressed debtor on the boundary line of adjacent counties, he may take refuge in the one element or the other as convenience may dictate. A political Preacher! bah!— . . . (May 24, 1839, p. 3).

MISCELLANEOUS

―――――――

I.

Dog Suit—A very interesting case was tried before his Honor Judge Pearson, at Stokes, the subject of which was the *felonious* killing of a dog with poison. The case was made out by the Plaintiff pretty clearly, and on the part of the Defendant it was scarcely denied, but that he did produce the death of poor *Sounder,* but they alleged some piccadilloes in the habits of the deceased, which they thought took away the cause of action. For instance, it was proved by Mr. Lockanour, that he caught him upon two sheep in one day. It was proved by Squire Aldy, that he was standing in his yard one day, when two dogs, Sounder and a black dog *with a short tail,* passed by him in company, and proceeding very deliberately to a hen's nest in the back yard, each took up an egg in his mouth, and came dashing back: as they passed the style he says, he gave the black dog with a short tail, a blow with his fist in the side, but he *proceeded on in his bright career.* The squire also proved that as he was walking the street of Waughtown, this same dog came poking up behind him, and snapped at his heels. To this it was replied, as the squire had lately put on a red wig with black whiskers, the dog, tho' a close neighbor, did not know him. After a very interesting argument in behalf of the Plaintiff, the cause was submitted by the defendant, and the Jury gave damage *one dollar.* The defendant has appealed to the Supreme Court. He insists that a *sheep killing* dog is of no value, and therefore, no damages can be given for its destruction.

There is an undercurrent in this affair, that caused it to produce quite a sensation. It is said that there was a damsel fair at the Plaintiff's house, to whom the defendant was deeply attached: that his passion was reciprocated, but that the family, and particularly the Plaintiff, was opposed to a marriage. They nevertheless had stolen interviews, and but for the vigilance of this dog and that of an old lady, who watched over her charge as faithfully as Dracon guarded the golden apples of the Hesperides, it is believed they would have made a runaway affair of it. It was with this view that old *Sounder* was removed. But alas, and alack, it would not all do; she is now the wife of another!! *Carolina Watchman,* October 20, 1838, p. 3.

2.

"Perley Poore," the editor of the *Watchman* wrote, "it will be recollected, engaged, in case Mr. Fillmore should not be elected, to roll a wheelbarrow full of apples from Newburyport to Boston, thirty-five miles; which he did in good faith, and was received in the latter City with many demonstrations of applause. We make no objection, at this time o'day, to the Fillmore vein that runs through our friend's verses. On the contrary, it is creditable to him as a man of spirit, that these poetic flashes shuld be seen through the cloud of defeat which rests upon his cause. We have always admired pluck and "grit" in an adversary—the more especially when they exhibit themselves like "orient *pearls* at random strung"—that is, in *Perley poore*-try.

PERLEY POORE ON THE ROAD TO BOSTON.
By H. C. Jones, Esq., of Salisbury, N.C.
Why Perley Poore, what is't ye mean
    By sic* a fasheous* splore*?
A wheelin' o' l'apples, sure my een*
    Ne'er saw the like before.

I trow* your hands are not acquent*
    Wi' sic toilsome work;
Ye're tired, maun*, and well-nigh spent—
    Besides, 'tis getting dark.

If gang* ye maun* wi' sic a load,
    I'll lend a hand mysel',
And tho' 'tis late, and rough the road,
    I'll try it for a spell.

Weel* neighbor, 'tis a foolish bout*
    A wager I hae lost:
I maun* redeem my word that's out,
    And never count the cost.

I waged wi' Burbank at the poll,
    The true and tried Fillmore
Would beat his man, or I would roll
    These apples to his door.

Now, whether it be right or wrang,
    The forfeit I maun* pay;
So wi' these apples I will gang*
    To Boston town this day.

That's the true spirit, honest wight*,—
    The right Whig grit* I ween*;
I'd rather lose in doing right,
    Than doing wrong, to win.

And if I live to vote again,
    Of course I'll go Fillmore.
But next to him, of living men,
    I'll vote for Perley Poore.
        Carolina Watchman, January 13, 1857, p. 3.

PART THREE

Stories and Sketches
Probably Written
by Ham Jones

INTRODUCTION

"Original Anecdote" appeared in the first issue of the *Carolina Watchman*. Joe Philips is a cracker* type, which Jones often wrote about, and the Billy Gaskins mentioned is a thinly veiled reference to William Gaston, Jones's teacher and friend. The repartee in the story, presented without authorial comment, is similar to dialogue in other Jones stories. Since the anecdote is not attributed to any other source, it was probably written by Jones.

"Lawyer's Office" is reported largely in dialogue form as was "Cousin Sally Dilliard," and appears to be a transcription of a conversation in an attorney's office. Kate Evergame, the woman complainant, does not object to being called a whore (that seems to be the word to go in the blank), but she does object to being called "slab-sided"* and "speckled-skinned."* Again, the story is not attributed to any other source and is probably Jones's.

"The Enchanted Gun" has to do with a practical joke played on a man who had been drinking heavily at a military muster. The political tag is completely in keeping with Jones's own antinullification views, and since the story is not credited to anyone else, we believe it is probably by Jones himself.

"A Buncombe Story" is probably one of the many stories that lawyer Jones heard as he traveled on the law circuit. It is more explicitly sexual than Jones's other stories. It is not signed, and we are attributing it to Ham Jones, as Richard Walser did.

ORIGINAL ANECDOTE

Retort Courteous.—Not long since, as a company of gentlemen entered the Piazza of a breakfast house, on Norfolk stage line, they were thus saluted by a fragmetical* fellow, who seemed to have been wresting hard all night with the jolly God.* Good morning Gents., My name's Joe Philips; I live two miles back from here: I'm very well acquainted with Mr. Billy Gaskins,* the great lawyer— and Galbe Hurard, and our member in Congress from these parts, and so forth, and so on; at your service, gentlemen. "Why" says one of the passengers, to another, in pretended undertone, but loud enough, nevertheless, to be heard by Mr. Philips, "this must be a pretty considerable man." "No doubt of it," says the other. "I see the marks of greatness in his right eye;" "smart man" says a third. These disinterested compliments evidently pleased Mr. Philips. He paraded a flourish or so of Rhetoric. He made divers efforts of wit, and laughed long and loud at them himself. His hearers seemed much to admire Mr. Philips, and were not at all sparing of their praises, all of which *accidentally* reached his ears. They spoke of his person; his gait (which was a little rolling); his wit; and the superlative cut of his coat. Mr. P. swallowed this "like sweetened liquor." He loomed, he swaggered, he bowed himself in ecstacies. "Talking about wit," says he, "let me tell you gentlemen how I cut Jake Simonds 'tother* day: Jake is allowed to be tolerable keen himself, and he and I was always a bully raggin* one another, and sometimes Jake would get the better, and sometimes I would.— One time, not long ago, some of my spiteful neighbors colleagued together, and indicted me for stealing of a shoat, and they took me down to that there place called _____ and there was one and twenty Lawyers employed to defend me, and it was all about Joe Philips and the shoat, and the shoat and Joe Philips: And I began to think they never would be done with it. There they had it for a whole day—Joe Philips and the shoat, and the shoat and Joe Philips—I began to wish I never had seen the darned thing. At last, I got so tired of the confounded fuss, I told the court if they would jest stop it, I did'nt mind takin' a small dressing.* You see I wanted to cut the Lawyers—Ha! ha! ha! So they took me out and tied me to a persimmon tree, and gave me thirty-nine lashes; but by Gracious I was not guilty of the shoat. And as I was going home, who should I meet but Jake Simonds, and he had jest come out of the Penitentiary—he had been put in for stealing of a sheep: Good morning, says he to me, Mr. Philips! good morning, says I to him, Mr. Simonds! "I understand" says he, "Mr. Philips, that you have been shaking down Persimmons lately;" "Well, by gracious" says I, "suppose I did, there was ne'er a sheep fell among 'em."—You see it takes me to do the thing; ha! ha! ha! Jake always let me alone arter that.

Carolina Watchman, July 28, 1832, p. 1.

Now this is fact and no poetic fable.—BYRON.

LAWYER'S OFFICE

CONSULTATION.
ENTER, KATE EVERGAME.

Kate—I have come in here Mr.————for to get you for to give me a writ for damage agin Mose Pennyfee, for the nasty scandalous talk he had about me—he has talken about my corracter for ever so long, and I won't take it any more.

Mr.———— —Did he vilify your chastity, Katy?

Kate—Yes that he did Mr.————. He bullified* my chestitee up and down and over agin.

Mr.———— —Well, what did he say?

Kate—Why he called me all sorts of mean names.

Mr.———— —You must tell me what he said before I can bring suit for you.

Kate—Well, he said I was a dirt-eating b————h and a heap more of such nasty talk.

Mr.———— —Well, what else did he say?

Kate—Why he said I was slab-sided,* cat-hamed,* hip-shoten,* wind-broken,* speckled-skinned,* and that my eyes looked like two holes burnt in a blanket.

Lawyer's Office Consultation

Mr.———— —Well, but did he say or signify that you were a —
————.

Kate—O yes, he said that over and over again, and said he could
prove it by forty witnesses—*but that I didn't mind.* I want you to
put in the writ about his aggrifying* my corracter. And when it
comes to trial, I want you to bemean him, and bullify his chestitee
jest as much as he did mine.

Mr.———— —I am afraid, Kate, your case wont bear an action,
unless you put in about his calling you a ————.

Kate—O me, what shall I do. (weeping.)

The disconsolate fair one was, however, pacified by the lawyer's
telling her that although he could not bring suit he could publish
Mr. Mose Pennyfee in the Newspaper for his pains, which is done
accordingly.

Carolina Watchman, August 4, 1832, p. 3.

THE ENCHANTED GUN.

It happened some sixty or seventy years since in the land of pumpkins, that an honest old simpleton who had been "to training," had made money enough by throwing stones at a "training cake"* to get very comfortably fuddled even without a draught upon his purse of the "four pence ha penny" laid up for that purpose several months before. Some wags who had kept more sober on the occasion than our hero, not having so good luck at the ginerbread gambling, loaded his gun to the very muzzle with alternate charges of excellent "double battled"* and *touch-wood**, starting him homeward, took care to put a red hot nail upon the topmost piece of touch-wood. Uncle Ichabod, honest old soul, shouldered the firelock, and took up his line of march for home. He had not got far, however, before pop goes the first charge from his gun—singular, thought Uncle Ichabod, but a mere accident, doubtless, a charge being left there carelessly. A few yards further, bang! goes the second charge—"Lard-Marcy," says Ichabod, "this is tarnal strange I swagger,* but I guess it did'nt all go off the first time, or else it would'nt go off again, would it though?" He had hardly finished his dialogue with himself, before off goes his repeater again.—"My gracious," exclaimed our terrified militia man, "the old boy is in the gun. I never *haird sich* a thing in my born days"—an exclamation which he hardly concluded before his everlasting gun struck four, and Ichabod, having no fellowship for a weapon possessing such fearful continuity of explosion, very prudently threw it over the fence, and made rapid strides for the house of a clergyman, having now no doubt that he or his gun was bewitched. The clergyman himself was not without his doubts on the subject; after Ichabod had testified to the whole story, the truth of which was corroborated by several distinct discharges from the gun in the place where he had thrown it, which was within hearing of the parties. However, while the matter remained sub judice,* the mischievous crafts who had caused all the alarm arrived with the offending musket, which made its last discharge in the clergyman's presence, and refused further services till re-loaded. It was never fairly settled, between him and Ichabod, whether or not, it was a real case of Witchcraft.— *"Nullifiers believe in Witches."*

Carolina Watchman, September 22, 1832, p. 4.

A BUNCOMBE STORY

> "But this that I am gaun to tell,
> Which lately on a night befel,
> Is just as true as the Deel's in H————l
> Or Dublin City." [Burns.]

A real raw of a chap went with his intended to Asheville to get license to be married, but the Clerk was not there; he lived a few miles in the country: so they did not know what to do. They were informed however, that Mr. C., a merchant in the place, delivered out licenses for the Clerk in his absence. Away they posted to the store and asked "if they had marriage licenses to sell there." The merchant answered, that he usually kept licenses there for the Clerk, but that the whole stock was exhausted. This was awkward again: the two lovers had a consultation—it was too late to go to the Clerk in the country, and there seemed no alternative but a postponement of the wedding: when of a sudden the gloomy prospect was cleared up—Dan Wilson, a merry Constable, saw that the Bridegroom was a flat*: he saw too, the awkwardness of their predicament, and beckoning the fellow to one side, he asked him who was to marry him. "Squire W." was the answer: "I can give you license," said the Constable. "Can you," said the countryman, and his heart leapt for joy. The writing was drawn, and it ran nearly thus,

"Old W———

You d———d old fool, you are hereby commanded to bind this Rascal in the bonds of matrimony with this b———ch, firm and tight, and be d———d to you. Signed,

Nobody."

Squire W———, a good, easy, conscientious man, lived in the border of the town of Asheville—thither the devoted two repaired and made known their business. The Squire simply asked if they had a license; on the fellow's answering that he had, he proceeded without further parley, to tie the knot; shortly thereafter, the effectual rite of *stowing away* (as the sailors have it) was duly performed. And now, we must for a while, leave the parties to their happiness, while we change the scene for a moment; and this carries us back to Asheville.—Dan Wilson was so full of his joke, that he whispered it first in one ear and then in another, until every wag of a merchant's clerk in the village had got wind of it—so after the stores were closed for the night and supper was over, several of them marched down to the Squire's to see how the thing had taken with him: "Well, Squire," says one of them, "we heard there was to be a wedding here tonight, and we have come down to see it." "You are too late," says the Squire, "the wedding is over and the parties are gone to bed." "But" enquired the spokesman of the party, "did they have a license, Squire?" "Why yes," said he, "I suppose they had—I asked the man and he said he had." "Well, but did you see it—it is well enough to look into these things—you know there is a heavy penalty for marrying people without authority, and we learn that the fellow did not have a license." "I did not see it," said Squire W., "but I *will* see it," accordingly he pushed into the apartment of the wedded ones, and presently brought forth a paper, which he commenced reading partly to himself and partly aloud, soliloquising as he read, pretty much thus: "Old W———" *"what's this, what's this"*—"fool," *I'm dished, I am tricked—ruined;* "bind this rascal," *"Dan Wilson, just like him,"* hum, hum, hum, "firm and tight,' *"yes, its Dan,"* "signed nobody." "GET UP," "GET UP," roared the Squire as loud as he could bawl, "GET UP"—"yo aint married—you aint half married—the license aint good: get up," and before the bedded couple could comprehend head or tail of the fuss, he rushed into the chamber, and seizing the first foot he could get hold of, which happened to be that of the man, he dragged him out of bed and left him sprawling on the floor—The result was, that the disturbed bridegroom had to ride off several miles to the Clerk and get a lawful warrant, whereby he was legally tied "tight and firm" about day break.

Carolina Watchman, April 16, 1836, p. 3.

PART FOUR

Stories Reprinted
by Ham Jones
in His Newspaper

INTRODUCTION

Ham Jones reprinted many stories during the years he edited the
Carolina Watchman, and this sampling is included to give readers an
idea of the kinds of humor that appealed to him. "Moustache" pits
country bumpkin against city fop, and in doing so deals humorously
with class distinctions and fashions. "Peggy Dwyer" is a curious
story, reflecting the racial prejudices of the time, but ending with
the "wronged" Peggy Dwyer out of emotional control and spending
the night in jail. The misspellings are comic, but the story is not.

"Scandal" is a set comic piece aimed at the gossipmongers found
in every village. Jones almost always avoided comic stories with an
overt moral, but the moral lesson in this story was one undoubtedly
familiar to and much admired by rural North Carolina readers.

We know from one of the Omnibus pieces that Ham Jones owned
a race horse and was fond of racing. It is in keeping with his
interests that he would publish a story about horse trading and
racing, with all of their deviousness and gulling. "Lazy Sam" is an
early example of an American horse trading story, and as was often
the case (in fiction at least) the cracker* outwitted the rich planter.
As far as we can determine, this rollicking story has never before
been anthologized.

"Cousin Sally Dilliard" was often imitated, but the author of "A
Borer Outbored" uses the repetitious telling of the Jones story itself

---

in a series of events and jokes. Ham Jones reprinted "A Borer Outbored" without comment and, we assume, with a straight face, in the *Carolina Watchman,* knowing full well that a large number of his readers were quite aware that he wrote "Cousin Sally."

MOUSTACHE

"His tawny beard was th' equal grace,
Both of his wisdom and his face."
Hudibras.

"What's them are* things growing out of your upper lip,
Mister?" asked a country Yankee of a coxcomb whom he met the
other day.

"Sar?" exclaimed the dandy, fiercely raising his rattan, and
bristling up to the interrogator—"what business is that to you,
sar?"

"Oh, no business of any consequence, to speak on," replied the
Yankee—"I jest axed for information, not being much acquainted
with them are things."

"Well, sar?" retorted the gallant, angrily, "what if you aint
aquainted with 'em? Must a fellow of your cloth have the impudence
to question a gentleman of mine?"

"Is that raally your cloth, Mister, or is it the tailor's?" asked the
countryman.

"The tailor's!" exclaimed the coxcomb, fiercely—"what do you
mean by that? Do you intend to insinuate that I steal! sar I'll
not—"

"Well, I thought as much," returned the Yankee, carelessly

sticking his hands into his breeches pocket, and standing still before the dandy—"I thought you never intended to pay for them."

"What is that to you whether I pay for them or not? Ha'nt I a right to manage as I please with my own tailor—to pay him or let it alone?"

"Why, Mister, that depends very much on what sort of a bargain you make. If your tailor agrees to let you cheat him, why, that's his lookout, not mine. But you ha'nt told me yet what you call them are things on your upper lip."

"Sar, you're an impertinent puppy, sar."

"So I heard you say. Now father, he's got a tarreyer dog—but he don't tarry much, I can tell you—he'll kill three rats in two seconds—but, as I was saying, father, he's go a tarreyer dog, that's darned rough and hairy about the mouth—but, Lord! he aint a circumstance to you. He'd cling his tail between his legs if he was to see you, and cry Ti-i! ti-i! and run to the end of the world without ever stopping. My gracious! how like the divil you do look with them are things."

"Look! why, sar, they are all the go now.—There's no finished gentleman now but what wears moustaches."

"Mustychers, do you call 'em? Well, by hoky, they are musty, and rusty too. They look very much like the latter end of our dog's tail, when he brushes it on the floor. Faugh! I would'nt touch 'em no more than—"

"Touch 'em sar, if you offer to put a finger on them, I'll cane you within an inch of your life—I will, sar!"

"What, with that are switch, Mister? I should'nt mind it no more than I should an oat-straw."

"Well, sar, touch my moustaches, and see if you don't get it."

"Touch your mustychers! Why I'd as lieve touch two old chaws of tobacker that have just been spit out. Touch 'em indeed! Why, Mister, I would'nt touch 'em with the tongs—I can't conceive, for my life, what should induce any human crittur to wear sich farned nasty looking things as them."

"Nasty looking! do you call 'em? Sar, you have no taste. Nasty looking, indeed! Why, sar, they are all the admiration of the ladies."

"Ladies ha, ha, ha! Ladies! They must have a queer notion, any how. But there are some women who are on-accountable fond of puppies and sitch like animals; and I've seen 'em fondle and kiss 'em, as if they were human critturs—But, Lord! I don't see how any woman could ever let her lips come within gun shot of yourn. Admiration of the ladies!"

"Do you question what I say, sar!"

"Why, Mister, I don't know what kind of ladies you have in the city, here. But one thing I can tell you—our country gals would'nt no more let you touch 'em than they would a toad—they're very particular what comes in contact with their lips. But, Mister, how in the name of hair and bristles do you eat? How do you go to work to git the vittles into your mouth, with them are things hanging over it, like a hedge-fence over the side of a ditch? Do you eat meat and sich like? or do you live upon spoon vittles."

"It's none of your business, sar, what I live on. I board at seven dollars a week; and I eat what I please, sar, and drink what I please."

"Seven dollars a week! my gracious! we git board and washing, and all, in the country, for a dollar and a half, but I speck they charge you five dollars and a half extra for them are mustychers. Faugh! I wouldn't have 'em at the table for ten dollars."

"D—n it! what a fool I am to stand there talking, with a fellow of your cloth." Thus saying, the man with the moustaches flourished his dandy switch, wheeled about, and walked on. He had gone but a few steps, when the Yankee bawled after him—

"Hullor! Mister—Don't you want a currycomb? I've got some real fine ones, with teeth on both sides. They're bang up, I can tell you."

"Curse on your currycombs and you too."

"Don't swear, Mister—nor go off in passion. I meant no offence in what I've said.—But I must declare you're the darn'dest ugly looking man in the face, I ever see in all my life."

Carolina Watchman, August 18, 1832, p. 4.

[PEGGY DWYER]

Peggy Dwyer, a plump, good-faced, good-natured girl, lives in South Street and takes in plain sewing. She comprises the whole of her family, and consequently has no care upon her mind, but that which relates to her own "welldoing" in the world. Peggy passes for a clever woman, and folks say she is an obliging neighbor, but she lacks spirit. Her reputation as a seamstress is high, and many are the applications which she has to teach the art of stitching to others, but no one as yet has been successful. Peggy has one answer to all such—"You likes my work, well—I learns your child, well—your child then does your work, well—you gives me no more, well—I won't have her, well."

Peggy lacks spirit. The unprincipled impose upon her—one borrows a needle, and never returns it; another her ball of cotton; a third her dripping pan, a fourth a half dozen potatoes for dinner. These things, it is true, cause Peggy some uneasiness for a moment, but her natural good humor soon returns, and the injury is forgotten. She however, on Saturday last, received a borrowing application which was too bare-faced even for "obliging Peggy," and summoning up resolution, she resolved "she'd do no sich thing." The application was as follows—

"Peggee Dire—

i takes mi pens in hand to lets you no as i goes to A partee this nite At tom Coles and Wants your New combe kause mines Broke an Wont do. SUSE BULLER."

Extraordinary as it may seem, it is affirmed by Peggy Dwyer that this application was from a negress! Peggy sent word back—"as she wanted her comb herself, [she] could'nt spare it," and thought no more of the matter.

Last night, Peggy, after tea, as is usual with her, took a stroll along the pavement in front of her door, to see what might be going on among her neighbors. She had not been sauntering long, before she felt some person behind her forcibly removing her comb from her nicely arranged hair. Quick as thought she turned to detect the thief—and, hurrying away with her comb, was Suse Buller, the jade, who sought that means of revenge for the affront. Peggy gave chase for three squares but fell short of overtaking the thief by one half the distance.—The vexation made her frantic, and she indulged in some remarkable queer capers—such as jumping, stamping, swearing, crying, &c. which in due time brought the watchman.

Peggy Dwyer spent the night in the watch-house.* This morning, after a severe reprimand, she left the office to prosecute Suse Buller for her comb.

Carolina Watchman, September 1, 1832, p. 4.

SCANDAL

"Now, let it work. Mischief thou art afoot,
Take what comes, thou wilt."

The substance of the following is no fiction.—In a neighboring village, whose inhabitants, like the good people of Athens, were much given to "either tell or hear some new thing," lived Squire P., a facetious, good natured sort of a body, whose jokes are even yet a matter of Village Record, and have been re-told through various editions, from folio down to duodecimo.

Aunt Lizzy was Deacon Snipe's wife's sister—a maiden lady of about fifty—she went to all the meetings—kept a regular account of every birth, death and marriage, with their dates—doctored all the babies, and knew every yerb* in the neighborhood—showed all the young married women how to make soap, and when they had *bad luck,* made every child in the house set *cross legged* until the luck changed. In fine, she was a kind of village factotum—spent her time in going from house to house, grinding out a grist of slander to each, as occasion required, but always concluded with "the way of transgressors is hard"; "poor Mrs. A. or B. (as the case was) I pity her from the bottom of my heart," or some such very *soothing* reflection. Aunt Lizzy was always very fond of asking strangers and others, without regard to time or place, "the state of their minds; how they enjoyed their minds," &c. These questions were generally followed by a string of scandal, which was calculated to destroy the peace and happiness of some of her best neighbors and friends; but she, like other narrators of this kind, considered such intellectual murder as either establishing her own fair reputation, or as the only mode of entertaining the village, and thereby rendering her society agreeable.

One warm summer's afternoon, as the Squire was sitting near his office door, smoking his pipe, Aunt Lizzy was passing by with great speed, ruminating on the news of the day, when the Squire brought her suddenly to, as the sailors say, by "what's your hurry aunt Lizzy? walk in." The old lady who never wanted a second invitation, went into the office, and the following dialogue soon commenced.

"Well, Squire P. I have been thinking this forenoon what an useful man you might be, if you'd only leave off your light conversations, as the good book says, and become a serious man—you might be an ornament to both church and state, as our minister says."

"Why, as to that aunt Lizzy, a cheerful countenance I consider as the best index of a grateful heart, and you know what the Bible says on that subject—'When ye fast, be not as the *hypocrites of a sad countenance,* but anoint thy head and *wash thy face* (aunt Lizzy began to feel for her pocket handkerchief, for she was a taker of snuff,) that thou appear *not* unto men to fast.' "

"Now, there Squire—that's just what I told you—see how you have the *scripter* at your tongue's end; what an useful man you might be in our church, if you'd only be a doer as well as a hearer of the word."

"As to that, aunt Lizzy, I don't see that you *'professors,'* as you call them, are a whit better than I am, in *private.* I respect a sincere profession as much as any man, but I know enough of *one* of your church, whom you think a great deal of, to know that she is no better than she should be!

At these inuendoes, aunt Lizzy's little black eyes began to twinkle; she sat down beside the Squire in order to speak in a lower tone—spread her handkerchief over her lap, and began to tap the cover of her snuff box in true style, and all things being in readiness for a regular siege of "scandalum magnalum,"* she commenced fire—

"Now, Squire, I want to know what you mean by *one* of our church? I know who you mean—the trollop—I didn't like so many curls about her head, when she told her experience."

The Squire finding curiosity was putting his boots on, had no occasion to add spurs to the heels, for the old lady had one in her head that was worth both of them. Accordingly he had no peace until he consented to explain what he meant by the expression "in private"—this was a *dear* word with aunt Lizzy.

"Now, aunt Lizzy, will you take a Bible oath, that you will never communicate what I am about to tell you to a living being, and that you will keep it while you live as a most inviolable secret?"

"Yes, Squire, I declare I won't never tell nobody nothing about it as long as I breathe the breath of life; and I'll take a Bible oath on it; there, sartan as I live, Squire, before you or any other magister in the whole country."

"Well, now, you know when I went up to Boston a year ago."

"Yes, yes, Squire, and I know who went with you too—Susey B. and Dolly T. and her sister Prudence."

"Never mind who went with me, aunt Lizzy; there was a whole lot of passengers—But, but—"

"None of your buts, Squire—out with it—if folks will act so—a trollop."

"But aunt Lizzy, I'm afraid you'll bring me into the scrape."—

"I've told you over and over again, that nobody never shall know nothing about it, and your wife knows I ain't leaky"—

"My wife! I wouldn't have her know what I was going to say for the world—why, aunt Lizzy, if she should know it"—

"Well, don't be afear'd, Squire, once for all, I'll take my oath that no living critter shant never as long as I live, know a lisp on't."

"Well, then—if you must know it—I slept with one of the likeliest of your church members nearly half the way up!!!"

Aunt Lizzy drew in a long breath—shut up her snuff box, and put it in her pocket, muttering to herself—

"The likeliest of our church members! I thought it was Susey B.—likeliest!—this comes of being flattered—a trollop. Well, one thing I know—'the way of transgressors is hard;' but I hope you'll never tell no body on't, Squire; for sartan as the world, if such a thing should be known, our church would be scattered abroad, like sheep without a shepperd."

In a few moments aunt Lizzy took her departure, giving the Squire another caution and a sly wink, as she said goodby—let me alone for a secret.

It was not many days before Squire P. received a very polite note from Parson G. requesting him to attend a meeting of the church, and many of the parish, at the south Conference room, in order to settle some difficulties with one of the church members, who, in order to clear up her character, requested Squire P. to be present.

The Parson, who was a very worthy man, knew the frailty of some of the weak sisters, as aunt Lizzy call'd them, and as he was a particular friend of Squire P's, requested him in his note to say nothing of it to his wife.—But the Squire took the hint, and telling his wife that there was a Parish meeting, requesting her to be ready by 4 o'clock, and would call for her.

Accordingly the hour of meeting came—the whole village flocked to the room, which could not hold half of them. All eyes were alternately on the Squire and Susey B.—Mrs. P. stared and Susey looked as though she had been crying a fortnight. The parson, with a softened tone, and in as delicate a manner as possible, stated the story about Susey B., which he observed was in every body's mouth, and which he did not himself believe a word of—and Squire P. being called on to stand as a witness—after painting in lively colours the evils of slander, with which their village had been infested, and particularly the church, called on aunt Lizzy in presence of the meeting, and before the church, to come out and make acknowledgment for violating a Bible oath! Aunt Lizzy's apology was, that she only told Deacon Snipe's wife on't—and she took an oath, that she would'nt never tell nobody else on't. Deacon Snipe's wife had, it appears, sworn Roger Toothaker's sister never to tell nobody on't—and so it went through the whole church, and thence through the village.

The Squire then acknowledged before the whole meeting, that he *had* as he told aunt Lizzy, slept with a church member, half the way up to Boston, and that he believed her to be one of the likeliest of their members, inasmuch as she never would hear nor retail *slander*. All eyes were now alternately on Susey B. and Squire P's wife—aunt Lizzy enjoyed a kind of Diabolical triumph, which the Squire no sooner perceived than he finished his sentence by declaring that the church member, to whom he alluded, *was his own lawful wife!*

Aunt Lizzy drew in her head under a large huge bonnet, as a turtle does under his shell, and marched away into one corner of the room, like a dog that had been killing sheep. The Squire, as usual, burst out into a fit of laughter, from which his wife, Susey B. and even the Parson, could not refrain joining—and Parson G. afterwards acknowledged that Squire P. had given a death blow to scandal in the village which all his preaching could not have done.

Carolina Watchman, November 17, 1832.

LAZY SAM

The following will not be worth the less for being true: A Kentucky horse-driver, being in South Carolina with a drove, happened to take it to the neighborhood of General H——, whose character for jockeying and manoeuvring in trade is much more celebrated than his feats in arms. The Kentuckian, having perfect acquaintance with his character, went to see him to sell him some horses, or to run a race, as the fates and destinies might order and decree.

He was one of your careless, unconcerned, knock-down and drag-out-looking sort of fellows, who would assume just as much simplicity of countenance and address as circumstances might require. He had the appearance of being about twenty-two or three years of age; as usual, was dressed in blue mixed jeans to hide dirt, and wore a drab colored hat for the same reason.

"Gineral," said he, "I am just from old Kentuck with some powerful nice horses, and may be you want some.—Daddy told me, if I come in your parts, to call on you, and he reckoned may be you would buy a pair of matches, or help me out in tradin': for he said you had a power of money, and understood tradin' to a scribe. Here's a letter from him," handing one. "And besides I've as nice a pair of matches as you could shake a stick at, and as tight a nag for a quarter, daddy says as any in the parts, but he says I must run no races, caze* mought* lose, and we want all the money we can scrape for land. But I reckon he'd suit you to a fraction, caze you are a sportin character, mought win a powerful chance of money with him."

While he was thus introducing himself and telling his business, the General opened the letter, which read as follows:

"*Dear general*—I take this opportunity to wright to you by my Job, who is taken the first drove he ever driv, and I want you to roll a log a leetle for him, if so be it suits you. Job's spry enough, but has'nt cut his eye-teeth yet, and if you will lend him a hand, I'll due as much for any of your boys if you've got any whenever they come to these parts tradin or any thing else. So no more at present, but remain your affectionate friend till death.

"PETER TOMPKINS"

The hero of horse-races, cotton-bags and sugar-hogsheads thought that he perceived a neat situation and acted accordingly. Mr. Job Tompkins was received with courtesy; his man and boy entertained with the best in the larder, whilst the five and twenty horses were not neglected. It is true that the General had not the slightest recollection of his friend and correspondent, Peter Tompkins. He might have once known him, or not. It was the same thing.—Here was Job, a raw Kentucky stripling with twenty-five horses, as easily squeezed as a ripe melon. It was not in his nature to forbear.

In the mean time, Mr. Job Tompkins made himself quite free and easy, and swaggered about the costly furnished apartment as if he had been in a log cabin. He viewed the silver plate on the sideboard with much astonishment, and a pair of silver-snuffers especially excited his curiosity.

"Lord! Gineral, ar them thar candle snuffers made out of the pure stuff? I never seed any afore but ir'n ones, and mammy uses her shears. And all them are things on that big chist (the sideboard) is the ra'al* Spanish castins? I heerd talk of this afore, but never seed it. Now, if I was to tell this in our settlement, may be they would'nt hop straddle me, and ride over me rough-shod, for a liar. But they said you're a powerful sight the richest man in the South States, aint you?"

To all which the General returned suitable answers; and Mr. Job and he were hand and glove for a successful lodgement in his

neighbor's pocket with a view of cleaning it out, a Herculean labor
to be sure;—when Job heard in the next room the sound of music.
Several Kentucky reels were played, anon the sweet breathings of a
melodious voice sung "Sweet—sweet home."

"May I be d——d," said Job, "If that don't beat Bob Walker,
and he's a patch above common! But that aint none of your music
boxes, I know: it can't be, is it?"

"My daughter is playing on the piano," said the General; "we
will walk in the room and hear her." Here were blandishments to
strike Job dumb and entrance all his senses.

> "The man who has no music in his soul,
> And is not moved with concord of sweet sounds
> Is fit for treason, stratagems and spoils."

Job thought a man might love music and spoils also. He felt a
liking for both. Therefore he applied the music in his own way
most rapturously.

Said Job, "May I never pull another trigger, if she's not a priming
above any thing I heerd talk about. Why she's chartered! She's a
ra'al one, I assure you. Why its enought to make a fellow swim that
can't; and if it was not for all these fine kiverlids over the track (the
carpet) and I had a partner to my mind, I'd go my drove to nothing
or less. I can shake the sticks off of any boy you can produce."

The General now thought the Kentuckian ripe enough.—To aid
in which he had been well plied with choice liquor, as he denomi-
nated the brandy and madiera.

The horses were brought out, and examined and praised and
cheapened, and faults found with all. They could agree upon
nothing.

"Well, where is your quarter-horse?" asked the General.—"Oh,
ho! I sort o' thought [it was] what you were after," answered Job,
"for you hardly looked at them thar matches, and these fine
geldings. So you must be after the quarter nag. Jim, fotch out Lazy
Sam, will you? Now, Gineral, I'll tell you, honor bright, he's never
been lickt in a quarterspurt but once; by Joe Miller's sorrel mare,
which runs like a streak of lightning. She's a real screamer. Daddy
swapt for him [Lazy Sam] last fall after she [Joe's mare]tanned him

out.* If I knowed her I'd give you her marks, so as you moughtn't be tuck in.—For I heerd Joe was bringing her to the South, to win his expenses. But here's the horse any how; and I assure you he's not slow."

Now be it remembered that honest Job was not ignorant that General H—— was, at that time the owner of this identical mare [Joe Miller's] and for reasons best known to himself, he wished to make a race between her and Lazy Sam.

The General examined Lazy Sam with the eye of a jockey.

"Pish!" said he, very contemptuously, "why this thing cannot run; it's as flabsided * as a sheep and as heavey shouldered as a hog, and cathammed* besides; I would not give a good mule for three of it. Why did you not bring a lot of mules to market? I would have bought some at a fair price. Your horses do not suit me. Pray what do you ask for this thing, which you call a running nag? It may do to plough a season or two. Does it work?"

Unlike the Job of ancient days, Job Thompkins suffered his anger to rise and master him. At least he made the General think so. To use his own words he corvorted—he screamed out.

"Hello! mister, I wonder you are so mighty wise, considering you know so leetle. Why you make me feel all over in spots, to listen to you. I reckon may be you've got a quarter-nag yourself, aint you?"

"I have got a plough-nag here," said the General very cooly, "that I am sure can runaway from that thing of yours."

"Thing!" hallowed Job, "Why you make me feel sort of wolfy,* and I've a good mind to go my whole lot agin any thing you can parade in the whole South."

"I would not spoil a good mind then," quoth the General. "I supppose you are afraid to run, as your father has forbid it."

"I dont care a solitary flint what daddy says when my Irish is up," exclaimed Job indignantly. "Bring on your nag, and let's see it."

The General gave the order; and as Job expected, the sorrel mare (once Joe Miller's) was brought forward.

While Job examined her, his adversary endeavored all he could to fret him, by dispraising his horse, and Job appeared to be worked up to fever heat.

To cut short the story, the drove was staked against twenty-five hundred dollars in a check upon the C——Bank—and the company adjourned to the General's track, to see the race. On the way, Job stopped short, and, facing the General, asked very earnestly,

"Now you're sure this aint Joe Miller's nag? My mind sort o' misgives me, caze, from what I have heerd, they sort o' favor like."

"D—n your Joe Miller and his nag also," replied the General; "the mare is mine, I tell you."

This appeared to be satisfactory. I have given the General's description of Job's running horse—done to fret him. Lazy Sam was a well made pony of the *Printer* stock, but of a mild, sleepy, sluggish disposition, until his metal was roused. He generally went with his eyes half shut and his head drooping at an angle of forty-five degrees. When the General viewed him he was in this condition.

The horses were in the General's Stable, and the check for two thousand five hundred dollars was in the hands of a gentleman present. The General had no doubt about keeping all Job's fine horses and sending him home on his ten toes. Job thought differently. Lazy Sam was led along by Job's boy as sleepy as usual. The preliminaries were adjusted, and riders mounted. As Job threw Jim on Lazy Sam, he sprang all fours off the ground; and his dull, sleepy look was changed into a wild, almost devilish expression. He looked like Job did when he *"corvorted."*

The General lost his usual mahogany color and became pale, but said nothing.

Lazy Sam won the race by thirty feet.

Job was suddenly cool as a cucumber—and as he put the twenty five hundred dollar check in his greasy pocketbook, which he did very deliberately, he looked round cunningly.

"I sort o' think that's first rate and a half," said Job, "and a leetle past common. Why, Gineral, Sam's laid you as cold as a wedge." Turning round suddenly to his rider, he said, "Jim, here's five dollars—why it all goes in a man's life time. And the Gineral looks as if he'd been squeezed through the leetle end of nothin, or less."

Carolina Watchman, July 12, 1834, p. 2.

A BORER OUTBORED
BY THE AUTHOR OF THE LAWYER
AND HIS CLERK

Everybody, I presume, has heard or read the tale of "Cousin Sally Dilliard," a fair specimen of irrelevant testimony given frequently by witnesses. To be appreciated it must be read, but to give an idea of it in few words: It appears that there has been a row at the house of Captain Rice, and a Mr. Harris is called on to testify, who, in the most prolix manner, gives a rigmarole evidence, commencing with "Captain Rice he gin' a treat,"* and ending after having said nothing about the subject, with, "and that's the height I know of the matter."

Jim Rell was a first rate fellow, heart and hand open: he had but little, but every one was welcome to a share of that. He was a lieutenant of our regiment, beloved by all the officers, old and young; but, when he chose, he could outbore any man under the sun, and when determined on fun—fun he would have.

I was some years since at the Post office with Jim, just after the arrival of the mail, when opening his paper he found the story referred to above; it pleased him amazingly, and, in a short time, every one in the garrison had heard or read it and Jim knew it by heart; however, it was at length forgotten.

Some months after, Captain Club gave a party, and conversation flagging, Adjutant Straw was urged to sing, when having complied, wine and cakes again made their rounds. All ladies of the fort and neighborhood were present, and, at my request, Miss Rick, the colonel's daughter sang; her execution was divine.

"Pray, Mr. Rell," said Miss Club, "don't you sing."

"Me, Miss!" replied Jim, "no never."

"You play on some instrument?" she asked.

"No, ma'am!"

"What can you do?" exclaimed Miss Club, pettishly, much annoyed by Rell's backwardness on two subjects in which she knew him to be adept.

There was a comick leer in Jim's eye as he answered—

"I can tell a story, if that would suit you."

"Do! do!" rose from every lip, when he, to their utter dismay commenced the direfully prolix account of the row at Captain Rice's. He improved on the original, and when an hour was passed, was no farther than "Captain Rice he gin a treat and my cousin Sally Dilliard come over to our house————."

"Don't for mercy's sake!" cried Miss Rick. "Please not to interrupt me!" said Jim in serious reproof. "Captain Rice he gin————"

"Mr. Rell," cried Miss Club, "I did not————"

"Captain Rice he gin' a treat and my————," said Rell.

The old colonel laughed, the officers chimed in—young officers should always laugh when the colonel does—and the ladies did the same out of pure vexation.

At midnight the party broke up, Rell promising Miss Club to call the next evening and continue the relation.

In this manner, day after day, Rell vexed this poor girl, till, at length, she was familiarly called by the officers, among themselves, "Cousin Sally Dilliard."

I remarked to my friend, it was wrong in him to joke the young lady so much.

"Not at all" said he; "she should not have tried to force me to sing or play, so snappishly, when she saw I was unwilling."

A short time after, Mr. Craig, a rich, kindhearted man [came] to visit us, and, being an old friend of Rell's, messed and lodged with him.

"Now fellows," said Rell one evening, just after retreat, as, in a squad, we were returning from parade, "come to my quarters after tea—old Craig has never heard the Captain Rice affair, and I'm going to let him have it; come in don't forget"; and we separated.

Craig was delighted at the story, and laughed so violently that we were forced to join him as soon as his merriment had somewhat subdued. Rell with a demure look, commenced explaining the story, while we, viewing the consternation of his visiter, were convulsed with laughter;—Craig did not know what to think; he twisted in his chair, laughed, and as suddenly looked serious; he glanced at us, then at Rell who had him by the button, and, in fact acted as any man would who was not certain whether he was being quizzed or not.

The indefatigable narrator so used up the story, by repetition, upon repetition, that his guests left, one by one, and I was the last; as I shut the door, to depart, I heard him telling old Craig the joke or point of his disastrous story.

Ere day had dawned on the following morning, Rell awoke Craig and continued his recital; the latter heard him patiently, at first— then impatiently, and finally fell asleep; but Rell was not to be defeated; he shook him lustily by the shoulder, and, as the sleeper opened his eyes, his ears were astonished by the words—

"Captain Rice he gin a treat!—"

"You have gone far enough with that joke," said Craig seriously.

"You see the beauty of it was," said Rell, "the witness did'nt say a word about the row; the court interrupting him, and then, telling him to proceed, he would invariably begin in the old way "Captain Rice he gin' a treat.""

The fact is, there like to have been some hard words; for Rell, being stubborn, was determined, as he had "bored" Craig out of humour to "bore him back again." But this was not to be; for the old gentleman, being dreadfully miffed, ordered up his horse and sleigh and bade us a hasty farewell.

It was a bitter cold day; the thermometor down to——, there's no telling how low it was, but off went Craig in a fury.

Just as he was out of sight, I turned to Rell and told him he had been too hard on his visiter.

"He had no business to get angry," answered he; "such friends as he and I should never fall out, and I have not paid him for it yet."

"What do you intend to do?"

"I'll see," he replied, shaking his head; "when he gets off four or five miles, I'll bring him back against this north-wester!"

In a few moments he called his servant, and feeing him with half a dollar:

"Jump on my horse," said he, "and gallop after Mr. Craig, and tell him business of the last importance demands his immediate presence.

Craig was full six miles from the fort when the servant, his horse covered with foam, overtook him and delivered his message. The unsuspicious old man turned about and drove back furiously against the cutting blast. We were all gathered on the piazza, and as the old gentleman saw Rell, he leaped from the sleigh, and running towards him cried—

"For heaven's sake, what's the matter?"

"Captain Rice he gin' a treat," said Rell, and the next instant Craig, horse and sleigh, were out of sight.

As we laughed over the affair in the evening, Jim remarked—

"I thought old Jack had more sense than to become offended with me."

Tattoo beat shortly after and we all retired to rest.

As old Craig rode on he reflected—

"How those youngsters will laugh at me. I was a fool for getting angry. I should have turned the joke on Jim," then turning his horse's head, the weather having cleared and moderated, he reached the fort soon after all were asleep.

Rell felt a hand on his shoulder and heard a voice—

"Captain Rice he gin' a treat" and opening his eyes he was overjoyed to see Craig, but during that night and for a week after, at all times and on all occasions, the latter never ceased this story.

Rell became sick and disgusted, but still the sound rang in his ear, "Captain Rice he gin' a treat."

By this course the "borer" became bored in return, & was soon

---

known by no other name than Captain Rice; but, being good at heart, he took it kindly.

Miss Club still bore her nickname of "Cousin Sally," and I believe this little incident, as much as any other, caused him to look with friendship on that lovely girl, and make the offer of his hand.

Shortly after the wedding I left the post, and had not seen Rell and his lady til the 28th of April, 1836.

I met the couple on the steps of the American Hotel, in Broadway; we shook hands and were making inquiries after one another's acquaintances, when a ragged urchin came by with a number of papers over his arm, crying, "Here's the Transcipt!"

I took out a copper and bought one.—On opening it, the first thing I beheld was an article headed: "Cousin Sally Dilliard!"

I handed the paper to Rell and his wife; the words struck them like lightning.

"The carriage is ready," said a prim, well-dressed negro, stepping up.

The two jumped in without even bidding me good morning, and as I walked away, I beheld the Transcript lying on the pavement, with the Cousin Sally Dilliard side up.

From the New York Mirror; reprinted in *Carolina Watchman*,
February 10, 1838, p. 1.

◆ G L O S S A R Y ◆

acquent   acquainted.

aggrifying   vilifying.

Alcott, Dr.   not identified.

ardent   distilled liquor.

Battle, Dr. Kemp   (1831–1919), was president of the University of North Carolina and university historian.

Battle, Judge William H.   (1802–1879), was a graduate of the University of North Carolina in 1820. He was a prominent attorney and judge and was a friend and professional colleague of Hamilton C. Jones. His son was Kemp Battle.

bout   fight.

Bottom   was Shakespeare's weaver in *A Midsummer Night's Dream*. Ham Jones was quoting Bottom's lines from memory; the lines should read:

> And Phibbus' car
> Shall shine from far
> And make and mar
>   The foolish Fates.

Words appearing in the glossary are identified by an asterisk the first time they appear in the text.

bull-beef beef from a bull and extremely tough.

bullified attacked.

bully raggin tormenting, teasing.

by Gracious a mild expletive.

Campbell, Col. William (1745–1781), was a hero of the Battle of King's Mountain. Long after his death, charges were made that he remained at the rear and did not lead his men in that battle. Those charges were never proven.

catamount puma; cougar.

cat hamed (or *hammed*) having flat haunches and crooked legs.

caze because.

chuffy fat, plump.

coal-wood charcoal.

corned drunk from imbibing too much corn liquor.

cracker a poor white in the Southeastern United States.

Crapeau a coined word appropriately French sounding; defecator (a variation of "crap"); a bullshitter.

double battled probably means double balled—that is, two musket balls.

dressing lashing.

Duberly, Baron not identified.

Duncans Kikkors possibly *Don Quixote*.

een eyes.

fasheous troublesome.

fipenny five penny; used derisively in referring to the amateur poet.

flabsided soft and with weak muscles.

flat dull; unable to read.

fragmetical broken, incomplete.

fuit probably a misprint for *fruit*.

gang go.

Gaskins, Billy A veiled reference to William Gaston, the noted North Carolina attorney and jurist.

ge-ep wae jolly not identified.

"gin a treat"   gave a party.

grit   spirit.

hath   hearth.

hip-shoten   having a dislocated hip.

Hyssops Fabbles   undoubtedly *Aesop's Fables*.

Jackson, Dr.   After the nullification crisis was over, Jones was once again opposed to the policies of President Andrew Jackson. A rival editor had obviously prescribed Jacksonian policies to the editor of the *Carolina Watchman*, and Jones was humorously rejecting that medicine.

Johnson, Dick   Richard Johnson (1780–1850) was Van Buren's vice-president. He was not married but had two daughters by Julia Chinn, a mulatto, who came to him from the estate of his father.

jolly God   Bacchus, the god of wine and revelry.

Kinderhook family   Martin Van Buren was born in Kinderhook, New York, and often referred to his family and his birthplace.

King Marty   Martin Van Buren, eighth president of the United States.

Loco foco   Democratic.

long-faced gentry   hogs.

lugged   fought, especially by pulling on ears and hair.

Man Preceptor   (man teacher) a madeup title indicating the ignorance of one of the literary society members.

maun   In "Perley Poore" the word is used two ways: in verse two it means *man*, and elsewhere in the poem it means *must*.

Moner Kumferted   not identifed.

mought   (also spelled *mout*) might.

nolens volens   willy-nilly.

"Obstupu-et steterunt que comoe et vox faucibus haesit."   He stood agape and his hair stood on end and his voice stuck in his throat.

paleface   liquor.

patrollers   Because of the uncertainty about the activities of blacks (both free and slaves) most North Carolina towns had a night watch. Citizens who made up the patrols stopped and questioned all blacks after ten o'clock.

pinchgut miser.

piney-woods-tacky a small, insignificant horse, descendant of wild horses along the North Carolina coast.

Pixe Rethmetic Pike's *Arthmetic*.

Plessurs of Hop a poem *The Pleasures of Hope* (1799), by T. Campbell.

Pol and Verginy a romance, *Paul et Virginie* (1787), by Bernardin de St. Pierre.

Pope's Asses Alexander Pope's Essays.

Porter, Mr. (and Mr. P.) William T. Porter, editor of *The Spirit of the Times*.

pressure depression.

ra-al real.

Racoon on the rail. "Settin' on a Rail" is reproduced in Lester S. Levy's *Grace Notes in American History* (Norman: University of Oklahoma Press, 1967), p. 95. The first verse is as follows:

> As I walk d out by de light ob de moon
> So merrily singing dis same tune,
> I cum across a big racoon,
> A sittin on a rail, sittin on a rail,
> sittin on a rail, sittin on a rail,
> sleepin wer-ry sound.

scandalum magnalum mock Latin, but the meaning is clear: "a huge scandal."

shaw a mild expletive.

sic such.

sine die for an indefinite period.

slab-sided flat chested.

speckled-skinned freckled.

splore frolic.

sub judice under consideration.

tanned him out   defeated him.

tarnal strange I swagger   mighty strange, I swear.

them are   them there.

Themis   the mother of Promethus; she summoned the assemblies of the gods and those of men. She was the goddess of justice.

throwing stones at a "training cake"   gingerbread ("training cake") was regularly sold at the military musters. The exact nature of the game of chance—probably using dice (stones) is not clear, but Jones is undoubtedly making a reference to the story in the Gospels of casting lots for Jesus' clothes.

'tother   the other.

touch-wood   balsam wood or kindling wood.

trow   believe.

Van Buren, Martin   (1782–1862), was a Democrat and therefore a political enemy of Hamilton C. Jones.

vicinage   vicinity.

want   wasn't.

watch house   a place where persons under temporary arrest are kept.

Wats Sams and hims   Psalms and hymns by Isaac Watts.

weasand   throat.

weel   well.

ween   believe, imagine.

wight   creature, being.

wind-broken   horse with pulmonary emphysema.

wolfy   aggressive.

Woodbury, Levi   (1789–1851), served as secretary of treasury during Jackson's administration.

yerb   herb.